SCM PAPERBACKS

now published

MEN OF UNITY *by Stephen Neill*
THE MIND OF JESUS *by William Barclay*
CRUCIFIED AND CROWNED *by William Barclay*
JESUS AS THEY SAW HIM *by William Barclay*
ST PAUL AND THE GOSPEL OF JESUS *by Charles E. Raven*
THE BIBLE IN THE AGE OF SCIENCE *by Alan Richardson*
INTRODUCING THE CHRISTIAN FAITH *by A. M. Ramsey,*
Archbishop of Canterbury
THE BRITISH CHURCHES TODAY *by Kenneth Slack*
CHRISTIAN DEVIATIONS: THE CHALLENGE OF THE SECTS
by Horton Davies
DESPATCH FROM NEW DELHI *by Kenneth Slack*
NEW DELHI SPEAKS: *World Council of Churches*
LOOKING AT THE VATICAN COUNCIL *by Bernard Pawley*
BEGINNING THE OLD TESTAMENT *by Erik Routley*
GOD'S CROSS IN OUR WORLD *by David L. Edwards*
CHRISTIAN FAITH AND LIFE *by William Temple*
WE THE PEOPLE *by Kathleen Bliss*
HONEST TO GOD *by John A. T. Robinson*

books which everyone can learn from and keep

D1464388

KATHLEEN BLISS

We the People

A Book about Laity

SCM PRESS LTD
BLOOMSBURY STREET LONDON

To Blanche Buttery

FIRST PUBLISHED 1963
© SCM PRESS LTD 1963
PRINTED IN HOLLAND BY
DRUKKERIJ HOLLAND N.V. AMSTERDAM

CONTENTS

PREFACE

THIS book began as a series of talks given to two clergy schools in the United States, organized by Dr David Hunter, director of the Division of Christian Education of the Protestant Episcopal Church. Most of my working life has been spent with lay men and women concerned to be Christians in the world of work, leisure, politics and community. It was for me an enriching experience to discuss the ideas and experiments made in other parts of the world with groups of American clergy from parishes as different as the suburbs of Boston and the mining villages of the mountains of Virginia. I am much in their debt, as I am also to my colleagues in the Church of England Board of Education and in the World Council of Churches.

In a topic so vast and so various much would be left out even in a large book, and this is a small one. Many others could be, and will be, written. But in the end of the day it is not what this or that person writes but how we act in worship, thought and life that matters, and I shall be delighted to hear that a record number of readers have thrown the book out of the window and got on with the job.

KATHLEEN BLISS

Oatscroft,
Midhurst,
Sussex

1

NEW LIFE FOR OLD

The Church Has Survived—For What?

IT has often been remarked that the Christian Church has outlived by many centuries all the political and social institutions of the world into which it was born nineteen and a half centuries ago. During this long history the Church has had some hairbreadth escapes from extinction by persecution or by foreign invasion; it has been at times suicidally divided, to the point of warfare between the parts; it has been stifled by patronage, corrupted by power, smothered by wealth, reduced by apostasy, split by heresy, immobilized by apathy, used and abused by the state, infiltrated by popular superstition, challenged by rivals. *Yet it has survived*. Some would explain this survival as the sheer inertia of ancient institutions which can look dead for so long without actually dying. Others will speak of the vast inherited resources of the Church—cultural, religious and economic—which it takes centuries to spend but which must run out some day.

To many, however, the present challenge to the Church has no parallel in history. It is new. It is universal, affecting every part of the Church in all the world. A Roman Catholic layman, writing on the eve of the opening of the Second Vatican Council, put the matter thus: 'The Second Vatican Council will take place in the context of two massive contemporary facts: (1) the growing threat of irrelevance that confronts not only the Roman Catholic Church but all Christian churches, and (2) the phenomenon of Christian Ecumenism.... The present threat to the Church of irrelevance and the present promise of ecumenism are distinctively modern and incontestably monumental.'

Few know this 'threat of irrelevance' better than the Christian layman, involved all day in the structures of the modern world from which the Church seems so remote. Is ecumenism 'a promise' for him? That is to say, are the churches learning *together* how to confront this threat?

If the layman seeks, as he must, to bring together the Christian faith and the modern world, he has to recognize at the outset the *double aspect* of the Church. On the one hand the Church is the divine community, called into being by Christ. This is its theological reality. The Church is part of the Christian faith. 'I believe in ... one Holy Catholic and Apostolic Church.' I belong to and worship in a particular church *because* I believe this, and not because social conformity demands it, or because I think the Church is a useful welfare organization. But, on the other hand, this divine community exists here on earth in the form of a social institution—companies of people meeting in buildings; orders of ministry regulating worship and doctrine; organized denominations; church institutions. This is a matter of *fact*, and the Church thus organized may be explored by historians and sociologists using the tools of scientific study.

Such study reminds us that God does not exempt the Church from the consequences of being a social institution. He does not keep it cosily in his hand, safe from change, decay and violence. He has always cast it out upon the world. The question of its survival as an institution in one particular form or time or place is an *open* question. There were once thriving Christian communities along the whole length of the trade route from Constantinople to China.

North Africa and parts of the Middle East were once strongholds of the Christian faith. They were almost entirely swept away by Mohammedan invaders converting at the point of the sword: the losses sustained were never recovered. A new Christendom arose among the barbarian tribes of Europe, a phenomenon no Greek or Roman could have imagined. And in our own time Europe may be rejecting its faith. Bonhoeffer reflects on the question: ' . . . if we had finally to put down the western pattern of Christianity as a mere preliminary stage to doing without religion altogether, what situation would result for us, for the Church?'[1]

In this time of ours three things are needed in the Church.

First, deeper theological thought about the nature of the Church as 'the divine community'. This theological thinking is going on actively today because churches have been coming out of their geographical, cultural and confessional isolation into living contact with one another through the ecumenical movement. Their confrontal has compelled them to ask 'What is the Church?' with new insistency and openness to one another and to the Holy Spirit.

Second, a more thorough use of the tools of sociology, social history and psychology, so that we see the institutions of the Church factually and not romantically (i.e. too rosily or too blackly!).

Third, a knowledge of, and response to, some of the new ideas emerging in the life of some churches or in their common action and thought. By ideas I do not mean bright ideas. I hesitate to call them 'movements of the Spirit' because that prejudges them before examination. Ideas have a history and cannot be understood apart from it. But

---

[1] Dietrich Bonhoeffer, *Letters and Papers from Prison* (SCM Press, 1953), p. 122-3. (Fontana ed., p. 91.)

I do not apologize because they are ideas. There is a general impatience in many circles with ideas, as an egghead's way of holding up action. However, the shape of our modern world has been very largely determined by what Karl Marx wrote in the reading-room of the British Museum. The ideas which I have in mind are ideas which seek to embody the spiritual purposes of the 'divine community' of the Church in forms of social life which are more appropriate to our time.

I have had the enormous privilege of visiting many churches in every continent, spending with them periods of weeks or months or (in India) years. What I write is therefore influenced by what I have seen and tried to understand. It is probably foolish to try to grasp and set down a sort of global picture of the situation of the Church in the world: yet I think that others would agree that while there are startling differences, there are also very large factors in common.

To sum up in advance: I am among those who believe that the Church everywhere *is* faced by a new situation, a new attack. But I believe that in these there is a new call of God to be faithfully (which means the opposite of 'inflexibly') his Church in the world.

Contemporary Attacks on the Church

There is an attack on the Church as institution. This is in very large measure an attack on privilege. Churches in the West, especially in Europe, have lost so much of what they once had of wealth and position, control over education, influence in the state, that they can hardly believe that they have any left. But every vestige of it, even the form devoid of much content, excites opposition. Sometimes this is resentment or even spite, but many regard the hangover of privilege as an encumbrance the Church can-

not afford to carry. In Asia and Africa the Church is suffering acutely from having come to these continents mainly
under the auspices of colonial powers. Few things are more
heartening than to see the struggles being made by younger
churches to divest themselves of, or suffer the forcible loss
of, the privileges that derived from their origin, and yet keep
the bonds of Christian love that tied them to churches in
the West. Sometimes the suffering—as in Ceylon—is very
acute. Only in the case of China has the break of the bond
with churches in the West been angry and—thus far—
almost complete.

The attack on the institution is also against authority.
The *ex cathedra* pronouncement, especially on moral
issues, provokes angry cries ('Who are they to tell us
what's right?'). One may even wonder whether within the
churches there is not a good deal of quiet ignoring of some
of the moral statements made from high authority. This
attitude of questioning authority is quite consistent with a
considerable willingness to sit down face to face with other
Christians and discuss the practical value of Christian
moral positions.

The attack on the authority of the Church in matters of
morals has a powerful weapon in the Church's own performance in various times and places. Indeed, there has
developed a sort of recital against the Church, continually
repeated and always with the same examples. It goes like
this. The Church is obscurantist (Galileo). It is class-
ridden and is on the side of privilege against the masses
(tolerance of slavery, failure to support workers in their
struggle for bread and human dignity in the industrial revolution). It is, in spite of its protestations, riddled with race
prejudice (South Africa and the Southern States of the
USA). On many important moral issues it is divided (war
and peace, divorce, birth control). Christians make claims

which they do not live up to and statements which they only believe by putting a very odd meaning to the word 'truth' (a charge with universal application).

A history of more than nineteen centuries, a world-wide Church, a broken Church, offer a target to the critic on which every shot can find a lodgement. Every accusation levelled at the historical Church is true of some part. Every Christian is bound to say, 'If thou, Lord, shouldest regard iniquity, who can stand?' Even while he winces at the short-sightedness of the critic, who sees in history chiefly what supports his case, he has to admit that Christians have often done the same, claiming for the achievement of the Church more than can be warranted by the facts. The critic, even when he is wrong-headed or ill-disposed (and he is often neither of these things), is frequently motivated by moral indignation: he is measuring the Church by a yardstick made in part by his own Christian heritage. The Christian can do no less: but he has also to understand the other source of the moral indignation directed against the Church. The critic has abandoned belief in man as, at best, a forgiven sinner. He says that the Church, if there is any truth in its doctrines, should not have fallen: the Christian cannot condone the offence, but he is bound to say that man falls and will fall and sins against his neighbour continually and that this, rather than the picture of man given to the modern world by the eighteenth century 'Enlightenment', fits better with the facts.

In addition to the attack on the Church, our time presents *in a new form* the attack on the faith which Christians have experienced from the beginning. Not for us the simplicities of armed invasion by the fanatical armies of Islam evoking costly but straightforward resistance: nor for most of us the bitterness of persecution calling forth the response of martyrdom. If science opens up a picture of the world which does not require God as an explanation of how things came to be what they are, this invasion of the mind by new ideas and concepts is not the work of enemy aliens—we Christians are among the scientists. Similarly, if our lives are invaded by technical devices liable to change things so basic as our kind and place of work and means of getting there, our leisure and where we spend it, and the size and spacing of our families—we are ourselves the technicians. The proverbial phrase about 'being in two minds' is true of many modern people; two ways of thinking and two outward cultures, one pre- and one post-scientific, seem to be embattled within one and the same person. It is important to be clear that neither science nor technology is itself the attack on Christian faith: but they provide the weapons. The main attack takes the form of an argument to the effect that the Christian faith belongs to a pre-scientific age; it answers questions which are no longer being asked; it speaks to conditions that no longer prevail; it addresses men in terms that assume God's existence and assume some need of him, whereas these assumptions can no longer be made. The questions whether the historical basis of Christianity will stand up to historical criticism, or whether it is possible, in the light of our knowledge of human origins, to think of human history as having a centre in a kind of invasion from another world represented by the Incarnation, deeply exercise many people. But many have given up thinking about them because it does not seem worth while, for even if the facts are as Christians say, they cannot attribute meaning to them. A friendly critic of the Church put it this way: 'Even if I had knock-down proof of the resurrection of Jesus Christ, I wouldn't know what to do with it: I wouldn't know what it means.'

Again the honest Christian has to admit how much truth there is in all this. There are books of Christian apologetic which start by elbowing the reader into a position of being allowed to ask only the questions the professional exponent of Christian doctrine can answer. A good deal of Christian propaganda gives the impression of having first to point out to people that they are not happy, or healthy, or useful: that there are snags, cankers, waiting disasters in their lives, and that it is to these rather than to felt, lived experience that the Gospel has a word to speak.

Not many of us who write and talk as Christians are prepared to face the possibility that there has been a real change of consciousness since the scientific revolution, certainly in the West, and probably wherever 'Western' knowledge spreads. By this change of consciousness I mean a change at a deeper level than can be reached by argument, of the way in which men *feel* about the world and their human condition. If it is true, for example, that man now looks at the universe primarily as something to be explored, with no limits, something of such absorbing interest that the imagination seizes on the facts and builds on and beyond them—which is what science fiction does— then this is something quite new in men's view of the cosmos. Again, if it is true that modern man simply cannot think of himself as man, the crown of God's creation who fell from grace and was shut out of Eden, but thinks instead of his place in the evolutionary scale, then sin and guilt cannot mean for him what they meant for his forefathers. Christians cannot effectively talk and preach as though Darwin and Freud had never lived and worked, and as though the results of their work had not seeped down into the consciousness of people who are not intellectuals at all.

The Church's Reactions

The reaction of institutions, as of most persons, under attack is to become defensive. Social forces have been at work cutting the many strands that joined the Church of a century and more ago to the life of the community. It used to be an institution in society to which every other institution was in some way related. It is now one institution among many. The Church has, to a large extent unconsciously, retreated within its own borders: *it has become itself a world*. How to break out again from isolation into communication with the world is becoming an urgent concern for many in the churches.

Meanwhile a far more subtle temptation than defensiveness has opened up for the Church, namely survival on the world's terms. It takes different forms in different places. American churches, for example, are assured of a secure future as part of 'the American way of life', if they are prepared to supply a halo of religious approval to the nation's picture of itself. 'How do you exercise a prophetic ministry to the nation when 62 % of the nation are inside the Church?' said one American minister aware (as are many others) of the dangers of the situation. In England the Church is happily tolerated as an Ancient Monument, 'part of our history', a piece of colour and pageantry on important occasions. Millions will listen to radio hymn singing, or join in 'Abide with me' at a football match. Far outside Europe the same danger of surviving on the world's terms exists. I once joined a vast pushing crowd of sightseers on the steps of a large Roman Catholic church in South America. It was 11 p.m. on a Saturday night. Every ten minutes a car or an old horse-drawn cab (the Indian features of the driver deadpan under a cockaded hat) drew up and a bride and groom—already married by

civil law—pushed through the crowd and disappeared
through the doors of the church. Ten minutes later they
passed on the steps the next couple coming in. 'No
sermon', I said to the South American friend who had
brought me. 'No sacrament either', she replied. 'How long
does this go on?' 'Till three in the morning—every week.'
According to statistics, not one couple in forty of those
married that night will enter a church again before a baptism or a funeral summons them. The Church can survive
as 'religion-as-such'—the garnishing of birth, marriage and
death with an aura of uncomprehended mystery.

But there is also survival of a wholly different kind—
patient, faithful endurance of suffering, persecution and
obloquy. I once read a letter from an Armenian woman
telling how in the periods of persecution which this church
has endured at intervals for centuries, the faith was taught
and Christian worship carried on in the homes of the
people. Some of these persecuted churches are teaching us
today that the will to survive on any terms is self-defeating, and that only response to the living God preserves and
quickens the life of a church.

As for the institution of the Church, so for the faith. The
sharper the attack, the stronger the instinct to 'preserve'
the faith, to keep it intact as verbal formulations although
the very language used has so changed in relation to our
present living experience of the world that the words no
longer mean what Christians really want to say. Thus
certain credal statements ('He ascended into heaven', for
example—but not this one alone, by any means) are no
longer explanations of what Christians mean, designed to
define their position over against the attackers (for in such
situations were the creeds forged), but are themselves
statements needing an explanation. Nor is the attempt to
preserve the faith by the liberal means of reducing it to a

hard core of less controversial statements any more successful, for there are no non-controversial religious statements any more. 'And was made man' raises not the question 'did it happen?', but 'what can it mean, what kind of a
statement is it, and what sort of a language?'. Nevertheless,
without ever having heard of Bultmann and demythologizing and other German theological mysteries, many
practical Anglo-Saxons do their own demythologizing.
They treat the creeds as a sacred repository of doctrine
which the clergy are meant to understand, perform their
religious duties, try sincerely to love their neighbours, and
trust in an unspecified way that God will take care of outstanding problems.

An alternative way of keeping the creeds intact as the
repository of the faith, and at the same time using something else to live by, is afforded by popular Roman Catholicism. Mary the Mother of God becomes the chief object of
devotion, the hearer of prayer, the intercessor. The faith
remains for clerical study: the believer does not need to
bother his head about the mysteries of redemption because
the Holy Mother plays in relation to them the role of the
mother in most families—immediately available, understanding, mediating. Nothing said in the Bible or the
creeds can be brought in to define or complicate this
simple approach, for there is nothing said. In Catholic
countries the wayside crucifix used to be a reminder of the
act of our redemption. This is who we are: the followers
of a crucified Lord. You will scarcely find a new crucifix in
Ireland: new and bright, the Holy Mother extends her
arms everywhere.

But there is a quickening in the life of the Church today,
visible over wide areas. It contains two elements—a response to the needs of men, and a return to search out the
roots of the faith and lay hold afresh on it as a living

reality. Whatever the critic may say in judgement of the darker pages of church history, he cannot deny that the Church has something of inestimable worth—a central point of recall. Christians have in certain circumstances been as rapacious, persecuting, indifferent and arrogant as other men, but always in denial of the central theme of Christianity—an act of condescending love by God to men, shown in all his dealings, and supremely in a human life given up wholly for men. Men turn back to this central theme of Christianity, usually under the stimulus of some outward pressure, some demand made by others which they cannot meet in their own strength.

Today, a needy world evokes from the churches a response of giving in money and personal help; the giving of such help turns men's minds to gratitude, to intercession, to an understanding of the meaning of Christian fellowship in much more than local terms. Similarly, the liturgical revival affecting many very different churches today is not unrelated to a growing realization that the Christian message in our day falls on deaf ears: our words seem to confuse rather than enlighten. It is hard to put our faith into words, but the acts of sacramental worship express what cannot be said and carry a power which words cannot convey. And there is the ecumenical movement towards Christian unity. This had its origins not within the churches themselves, but in their missionary encounter with Asia and Africa. It stands now, perhaps, at the moment when, after fifty years, it must itself be renewed before it ossifies into inflexible organizational structures. We have not begun to explore more than the shallows of its possibilities.

This book is about the quickening of life going on in many parts of the Church and many countries through the gradual recovery of a far deeper, more theologically grounded conception of *the calling and ministry of the laity*. This lay movement owes something to the state of the world, something to the liturgical and ecumenical movements, something to the separate traditions of individual churches. Perhaps under the Holy Spirit it may help to lead us out of an existence as Christian survivors, refugees from an alien world, into being in our generation bearers of life *in* the world.

2

THE LAITY: A RENEWED CONCERN?

THERE is no doubt that the question of 'the laity' is being widely discussed in the churches. One can scarcely pick up a magazine or a conference programme without seeing 'the vocation of the laity', 'the use of the laity', 'lay witness'. The discussion is going on in some form on every continent and in churches of every confession. The World Council of Churches' Department on the Laity has, for example, produced a list of 300 articles and pamphlets on 'the laity' in English, French, German and Scandinavian languages, and this is only a selection from a far greater mass of material.

What does it all amount to? There are very many strands, and we must try to distinguish them from one another.

1. *The traditional lay offices and lay functions in the different denominations and confessions*

An interest in these has been quickened by conversations between churches about possible re-union. In England the Presbyterian eldership has come in for a good deal of notice since the Anglican-Presbyterian conversations.[1] It seems incredible that churches should live as close to one another geographically as they have done for years in every city in England, and yet know so little of one another's structures and lay offices, that things long

---

[1] See, for example, the advocacy of its grafting into the Church of England, by a committee of the Northern Convocation in 1959.

known in one church can be greeted as a discovery in others. Anglicans knew astonishingly little about Presbyterian eldership before these conversations, and some have been keenly interested in what looks more like a New Testament 'deacon' than the embryo-priest of the Anglican diaconate. That the eldership should be an *order* in the church, genuinely lay; that the elder should exercise a pastoral ministry, under the minister, within the congregation; that there should be elders in all the levels of church government ('church courts') up to the highest (the General Assembly), covering every range of subject and decision—all this has been 'news' to most Anglicans.

Lay preaching, and lay assistance in the conduct of services, have also been much discussed. The modern revival of the ancient office of lay reader in the Church of England dates back to 1866. There is not much to be said in commendation of lay preaching not already said by John Wesley and his immediate associates, or experienced by Methodists in the last two centuries. Seven out of every ten Methodist services held on a Sunday in Great Britain are conducted by lay preachers. When, some years ago, a group of Anglican priests wrote with enthusiasm of the 'parish meeting' in which the whole congregation shared with the priest the spiritual, pastoral and material concerns of the parish, a group of Congregationalists showed a point by point parallel with the Church Meeting common in Congregationalism for four centuries. Similarly, discoveries of the freedom of lay participation which is afforded by liturgical structures are only *re*discoveries of the experience of the Church in the earliest centuries of its history.

The relation of lay leaders to the conduct of worship, especially eucharistic worship, is something that needs more study. The outward form of Presbyterian, Congregational and Baptist services of Holy Communion is very like a picture of the Last Supper—a table spread with a white cloth, behind which the minister stands and round which the elders or deacons sometimes sit. In silence they carry the consecrated bread and wine to the people: this is their role. In Anglican churches on occasions when there is a large number of communicants and too few priests, a licensed lay reader may administer the cup with the words: 'The Blood of our Lord Jesus Christ, which was shed for thee, preserve thy body and soul unto everlasting life. Drink this in remembrance that Christ's Blood was shed for thee, and be thankful.' Here, the lay reader plays exactly the role of the ordained deacon. He does not in any sense represent the people or fulfil a characteristically lay role.

It would be valuable to have a full picture of the many ways in which the Holy Communion is, physically speaking, celebrated, for each presents a visual picture to the mind of the worshipper. The role of any lay leaders is clearly important. In some contexts they seem to represent an apostolate called out from among the congregation, sitting as the disciples did at the Lord's Supper, and walking round giving to the people (spaced often 'in companies' to allow movement through the congregation), like the Twelve among the crowd at the feeding of the five thousand, which was also a eucharistic meal.

There have been suggestions that the cause of church unity would be forwarded if churches accepted into their systems the forms of lay initiative found in others. One can see the attraction of this, in that it seems to have a sort of ecumenical sanction to it. But it has also a certain artificiality about it, and it is difficult to see how such grafting could go on without either jettisoning what each church already has, or multiplying offices, orders and organizations in churches which, some would say, have too many already.

2. *Other forms of lay service within the congregation*

Elders, deacons, stewards, churchwardens, sidesmen, lay readers, lay preachers—all have duties towards the whole congregation or, in the case of the last two named, to more than one congregation, if authorized. But churches have many other functions for lay people, some of which have been built up by emphasis on training, examinations, etc., into functions demanding at least some standard of knowledge of the Christian faith and the Bible. Sunday School teachers are one example. All lay readers and lay preachers are expected to study. The leaders of most of the voluntary organizations in the congregation normally have no training. Congregations proliferate jobs: there is something for nearly everybody. Some churches regard this as an ideal; everybody *ought* to have a job *in* the congregation or *in* an organization, whether it is magazine delivery or piano playing in the kindergarten of the Sunday School. It is interesting that from very early times—at least the third century—'jobs' have hardened into 'offices' among the laity, with their own hierarchy of acknowledged importance sometimes.

This area is one in which Christian stewardship has really stirred up the waters. The calling together of a large group of men in a congregation, the careful explanation of the aims and objects of a stewardship campaign, the planning of a parish supper to launch it, the preparation of each visitor to handle the situations he will have to meet, have had some remarkable effects of a non-monetary kind —indeed, these are by far the most important. For many men this was the first time of doing something for the congregation which involved them in going out to meet other people and face the possibility of questions and explanations. Simple though it was, a little training had a great effect. The largest result has been the number of men coming forward with the double request, 'Give us a job and train us to do it'. This has taken many clergy by surprise. What does one give a man to do, especially if one has never really given serious thought to the possibility of so many requests for work? A stewardship of time and talents has therefore gone with stewardship of money. In the flood of requests for lay training received in the Church of England today the greatest number come as a result of stewardship campaigns, and this training includes as a main element training in group relationships and training in understanding of the faith. For what the laity lack is not the know-how of successful magazine distribution, but basic equipment in understanding what it means to be a Christian. 'I would like to have done my confirmation preparation all over again at 18 and then perhaps at 23: you don't take things in by just being told once.' Such a remark shows how continuous real training for Christian commitment has to be. There are in the churches many lay people waiting to have their real capacities released into work for which they are properly prepared. Some are finding it, others are not, and the Christian stewardship movement has done a notable service in preparing the way.

3. *Lay participation in church government*

The English Free Churches are always reckoned to have been among the most important seedbeds of English democracy. There is nothing in the Church of England to compare with the responsibility accepted by the *whole* congregation for the *whole* life of the local church in churches where a congregational order is fully operative. Social change has made for greater interdependence in

'Independency' and strengthened the powers of the Union and the Moderators.

Methodism is the most highly organized system of church government: it is an amazing tribute to John Wesley's organization that what he organized as a society should so easily have taken over the ordering of all the functions and disciplines of a church. In spite of the emphasis on lay preaching and witness in Methodism, the church as a 'brotherhood of ministers' is a very strong element in its government. Its supreme authority, Conference, is organized in two sessions, 'representative' and 'ministerial', and to the latter certain matters are reserved.

In the Church of England two systems sit uneasily together: the new democratic structures set up under the Enabling Act of 1919 bring the laity into full partnership with the clergy at every level from the Parochial Church Council to the National Assembly: but all control of doctrine remains with the two Convocations, each with its upper and lower house of bishops and proctors in Convocation (clergy) who also form the house of clergy of the National Assembly. Discussions are now going on about the possibility of establishing 'synodical' government, involving the laity in doctrinal decisions.

It is clear that so long as there is a *full-time* ordained ministry the bulk of the work of making the government of any church run smoothly will fall on the clergy. The main business of every agenda is the ordering of the internal life of the church, in which the clergy are the responsible leaders. The relationships of the church to the world are matters that appear less regularly and less happily. There is an inescapable difference between the two ranges of subject matter. If a church wants to sell its property, or expand its youth work, it can take a decision in the appropriate legal form and in due course the thing is done. But if it

wants to discuss something happening in industry or international affairs it inevitably speaks from the outside; if the
debate is on a resolution and leads to a vote, the decision
cannot be of the same kind as one affecting the affairs of
the church itself. It can approve, deplore, commend, etc.,
or it can ask someone else (perhaps a committee) to study
or consider the matter. There is always a feeling that this,
after all, was words not leading to action, in spite of the
fact that many true and wise things might be said in the
course of the debate. It may have its best results if the layman who knows from the inside the situation under discussion is able to make the kind of speeches that do a little to
inform or educate others. But his presence in that assembly is due to the role he plays in his local or regional
church; he is not chosen because he is a trade unionist or
an expert on foreign affairs—these facts about him are
fortuitous in this context. He may be the only person present who knows at first hand some social or political situation: the danger then is that he may be treated as far
more of an expert than he really is.

One is driven to the conclusion that deliberative bodies
with power to make effective decisions on the church's
internal affairs are not in their present form the best places
for discussing the world. Yet where else in the churches
can this be done, and where can the layman say to the
church what he knows and get the spiritual counsel he and
others need? We need, perhaps, purely deliberative occasions, or something like the old Church Congresses
when laity, not having any powers, sat down in a free
relationship with clergy and all read papers, exchanged
views and educated one another and said their prayers and
worshipped together. This would not take the place of, but
would help to inform, authoritative rulings on principle by
lawful church authority.

4. *Lay calling and ministry in the world*

On Sunday evening the last service of the day is over at
St Agatha's and at Wesley Memorial down the hill. The
last 'good-nights' are being said and the verger/caretaker
sees the vicar/minister out of the vestry, puts out all the
lights, and locks up. All day congregations have been
gathering in these and other church buildings to worship
God in Christ. Where is the Church now, and where will it
be at 11 o'clock on Monday morning? Not non-existent,
but scattered in schools, offices, factories, homes, over a
wide radius: *and still it is the Church.*

In more and more churches all over the world this presence of the Church scattered through the institutions of
secular society is being taken with increasing seriousness.
For years talking about the laity has meant talking about
their place in the Church gathered for worship, instruction and government: now it means talking about their
calling to be the Church in the world. At last the fact that
the layman spends the main part of his time in industry or
commerce or television is being treated as something more
than incidental. But he is not being talked of as the individual solitary Christian. The word 'laity', a corporate
word, is being used, even by churches which have never
used it before. This 'scattered' Church is being discussed
theologically; it is being studied sociologically.

The emphasis on laity has a history, which helps to explain what it is. The same concern with this presence and
ministry of the Church in the world through the laity is to
be found in the Roman Catholic Church (where much the
best sociological study has been done), and in many other
churches, to whom the main interpreter and stimulus has
been the ecumenical movement. Many of the things which
constitute a 'recovery' of emphasis on the laity in the West

are present as long-standing features in Eastern Orthodoxy. It seems genuinely to be a concern of the whole Church, expressing itself in different and mutually enlightening ways.

Instead of being exhorted to live as a Christian and, as it were, thrust out into the world to do his best on his own, the layman now has more confidence that his lay situation is being better understood in the Church. All the laity of all churches are in a common situation in the world. Wherever he works, wherever he meets the community at large, he finds that Christians are in a minority. His faith comes under fire or is ignored, or even pitied. He is regarded often as a relic of the past. When he goes to church that past comes alive, he hears, speaks and sings its language with sincerity and it becomes for him a vehicle of eternal realities. But he is conscious, acutely or vaguely, that all sorts of ideas about man and the world, hidden in the words, are of the past, belonging to a pastoral or patriarchal society, and to a triple-decker view of the universe. Instead of making sense of the world for him, the Christian's faith, couched in this language, is often a problem he himself is trying to make sense of. Yet he needs it to guide and sustain him in the world.

There is also a discontinuity or lack of organic connection between the Church as an institution and the rest of society. This is often spoken of as though it were a problem of the clergy having their pastoral and educational work taken from them by social workers, personnel officers, teachers and others. A distinguished committee of the Church of England produced in 1902 a report on 'The Position of the Laity in the Church'. This report has a closing chapter on the nineteenth century which makes it abundantly clear that the real changes were in the status and function of the laity who, by successive enactments of

Parliament, were deprived of the duty and responsibility of relieving the poor, educating the young, and administering church finance. One by one the institutional links binding the established church to the community were cut. The results the report summarized thus:

'The legislature has withdrawn from the Church the responsibility, and to a large extent the opportunity, for the performance of duties which of right come within the province of the Christian laity: and has by its legislative measures made it clear that in England "citizen" and "churchman" are no longer convertible terms, that a "parishioner" is not now so called because he is a member of the Church within a given ecclesiastical area, but because he is a ratepayer in a particular locality; thus compelling the Church to readjust its relations to the civil power, and to find a definition of membership which in this country was unnecessary before.

'The position is entirely altered from what it was 300, or even 100 years ago. These alterations are in some cases beneficial, and in others necessary; but the position, so altered, is one that is new to the Church of England; and it is this new position which we have to face, these new conditions with which we have to deal.' [1]

---

[1] The 1902 report by a Joint Committee of the Convocations was an important landmark in the achievement by the Church of England of its self-governing bodies, granted to it by the Enabling Act of 1919. But it was not the starting point of concern about the role of the laity in the Church of England, as the following list of reports of committees of the Convocation of Canterbury, with their terms of reference, shows:

1857 *On Lay Co-operation*. To consider 'the best means of obtaining the counsel and co-operation of the laity of the Church in Annual Visitations or Diocesan Synods or in any other modes that may be deemed expedient'.

1864 *On Lay Agency*. 'To consider the expediency of authorizing, by licence of the Bishop or otherwise, lay teachers to assist incumbents in house-to-house visitation, in catechizing, and in

This sustained emphasis on the laity helped to create the immense Church of England Men's Society of the early years of this century, and the Life and Liberty movement to which William Temple devoted so much energy. The objective of the latter was to free the church of unnecessary parliamentary control and to give the laity a voice in its affairs. One cannot escape the impression that this larger share was regarded as some sort of *compensation* for loss of the connection between church and society described above. The disease was rightly diagnosed—but the cure was doubtfully the right one, great as were its merits on altogether other grounds.

The English Free Churches reached the same situation of discontinuity between church and world by a different route. They never had the legal responsibilities devolving on the national church through the parochial system, but they did develop important organs and institutions of their own which met community needs and forged links between them and society. Until 1870 they, like the Church of England, supported church day schools; their Sunday Schools, programmes of adult education, and the work of some of their outstanding ministers and laymen for social betterment, were important forms of community service.

performing such religious services as may be assigned to them by competent ecclesiastical authority.'
Thereafter lay co-operation was the subject of a number of reports referring to parochial councils, diocesan conferences, provincial church councils. These were also tried out in practice. Over the same period a series of annual Church Congresses (the first in 1861) drew together clergy and laity to discuss matters of moment in the Church, including on a number of occasions the role of the laity. Nor was this concern just with 'machinery'. Questions of evangelism, religious education, and social work were debated. The theological aspect of the role of the laity was also taken up, e.g. by Moberly in his Bampton Lectures, *The Administration of the Holy Spirit in the Body of Christ* (1869).

Their most spectacular achievement during the nineteenth century was the development of political influence centring on a powerful group of Free Church laymen in the House of Commons. By the time the Church of England committee was producing the report just referred to, ministers of the Crown could be made to writhe under castigations from Free Church pulpits and look anxiously to see what *The British Weekly* had to say of their policies before they could breakfast in peace. Without any legal enactments to force the pace, the Free Churches experienced a similar cutting of the links between themselves and society.

As a result, all churches, Anglican and Free Church alike, have become increasingly engaged with an inner group of attenders. Providing for its pastoral care, religious education and social fellowship has absorbed time, money and interest. Evangelism has been conceived as enlarging that inner group or even sometimes as preventing those already in it from drifting away.

It is an interesting fact that until the middle or late nineteenth century church buildings were literally churches, places of worship: the only addition was the vestry. Halls and classrooms, kitchens and cafeteria are newcomers to church architecture. Their erection and upkeep, and the maintenance of the organizations that use them, absorb a large part of the gifts and time of the congregation. One simply cannot imagine a thriving local church without them. Yet how are we to evaluate them? Are they the spiritual base and power house for a laity acting in the world: or do they have the effect of imprisoning the laity in church structures? This is a sharp expression of one aspect of the present lay question.

The most significant signs of uneasiness as to whether the Church in its gathered activities is really upbuilding the layman for his life as the Church in the world is coming from places where the local church is prosperous, well frequented and busy.

'Our local churches', writes one American church leader with a wide knowledge of American congregations of all denominations, 'minister to the conscious needs of their own members.' Another speaks of the 'social irrelevance of the local church'. 'The individual Christian', he continues, 'gives of his means to people and causes; but along with this there can be, and often is, blindness to what the same individual does as citizen and worker in his community and occupation.'

Another, a Methodist minister in Texas, tells the story of the success and failure of a local congregation in a new suburban area. 'At the first service of the new church', he writes, 'sixty members joined, and by the end of the fourth year the congregation numbered five hundred. There was never any question as to our mission. Our mission was to build a new Methodist church in that town. Around this mission we developed what I would call an almost phenomenal relationship with one another. When we met as a committee there was an amazing percentage of the membership present, and they participated actively. We met all our financial obligations, built buildings and grew numerically. From outward appearance there was no question but that we could be labelled as a success. At rare times in my ministry there I knew that very little was happening at depth. There seemed to be little relationship between our faith and our personal lives. Problems, business and personal, confronted us, with little evidence that we approached them as self-conscious Christian people. At the end of the fourth year I had to leave, inwardly bitter about my fate, but utterly incapable of carrying on within the pattern which I had created for myself within that ministry.'

The lay question, in the form of lay vocation and ministry in the world, has therefore got little to do with whether we belong to one denomination or another, whether our congregation is large or small, rich or poor, or where it is in the world. So we ought to expect that a problem which is not peculiar to one church or situation has been an object of study and discussion between the churches and within the ecumenical movement, and that we can look to that quarter for help in our situations. This has indeed been so: in fact, the renewed concern with the laity in the world has its origins in the missionary outreach of the Church. The lessons learned there, discussed between the churches, illuminated the situation in the so-called 'sending' countries. But this was only because certain men did the things they did; and to these we now turn.

3

THE WHOLE CHURCH IN THE WHOLE WORLD

The Meaning of Ecumenical

'WHY can't we have an easily understood English word instead of a Greek one that nobody understands?' This is often said by people who (presumably) talk about photographs, telephones, antibiotics and geography, and therefore use words of Greek origin freely and unselfconsciously. The word 'ecumenical' is used because there is no other: but that is the least good reason for using it. The word itself has made its users think: think of the past, what it meant: think of the present realities and spiritual experiences it describes: think of the future and of the hopes that it embodies.

'Ecumenical' is both very old and very new in use.[1] The *oikumene* in Greek meant 'the whole inhabited world': the word was used by the historian Herodotus in the fifth century BC and by the authors of the Greek translation of the Old Testament, the Septuagint. 'The earth is the Lord's and the fullness thereof: the *oikumene* and they that dwell therein'. The New Testament uses it in the same sense: it is the place where the Gospel is to be preached. It was the *oikumene* that the apostles were accused of turning upside down (Acts 17.6). Origen (second century AD) used the

---

[1] In what follows I owe my facts to Dr W. A. Visser 't Hooft's Burge Memorial Lecture, *The Meaning of Ecumenical* (SCM Press, 1953).

term with a slightly new sense. A place where the Gospel has been preached is already a modified, a different *oikumene*, just because the Gospel has been preached in it. It is becoming, he says, the *oikumene* of the Church. He stresses again and again the function of Christians as salt in the world and the Church's responsibility for the 'conversion of the world'. One may pause at this moment to comment that Origen, living in a pagan world under a pagan Emperor (his father was martyred), here describes with his use of the phrase 'the *oikumene* of the Church' a typical function of the Christian laity, which is to make the influence of the Gospel felt in the ordinary conversations and structures of daily life.

In 312 AD the Emperor Constantine was converted to Christianity. This set in motion the forces that were later to bring so close a connection between Church and State. The first of a succession of what came to be called 'ecumenical councils' was called together by Constantine. His concern was, he said, 'to unify the mind of all peoples concerning the divine' and to heal the divisions and wounds in the empire. The Church did not, however, come to regard every Council summoned by the Emperor as an ecumenical council; and it did call 'ecumenical' some councils at which not all churches were present. 'Ecumenical' came to mean in the Church 'universally valid', and councils whose decisions and doctrine were such were regarded by the Church as binding and authoritative for the whole Church. Some people have therefore spoken of the Apostles' and Nicene creeds as 'the ecumenical creeds', because they were regarded as valid by, and regulative for, the Church.

What makes the word 'ecumenical' so valuable today is that it holds together things that must not be separated. It refers at once to the *whole* Church and to the *whole*

world. 'An introverted ecclesiastical ecumenism', says Dr
Visser 't Hooft, 'is therefore self-contradictory'. It contains all that is meant by 'Catholic' or would, if Catholic
had more overt reference to the presence and mission of
the Church *in the world*. 'Ecumenical' means more than
'universal', and far more than 'international' on the one
hand or 'interdenominational' on the other.

The recovery to the word of its full meaning has been
piecemeal over the past 150 years. Today the phrase
'ecumenical movement' is not a synonym for the World
Council of Churches or any other organization. Nor does
it describe what is already achieved. It is a movement
seeking after the unity of Christ's Church and the fulfilment of its purpose in the whole world. The word
'ecumenical' began to come back into use in the early
nineteenth century as a result of the evangelical revival. It
was used in the 1840s when the first explorations were
being made which led to the formation of the Evangelical
Alliance. Germans and Frenchmen first used it, and at
the conference constituting the Alliance, held in London
in 1846, British and Americans followed suit. The basis of
the Alliance was called the 'ecumenical basis' and the
conference report makes it clear that what was in mind
was the *spirit of unity* felt among the delegates in spite of
their national differences.

From the Evangelical Alliance the word quickly passed
into the vocabulary of some of the leaders of the YMCA,
which was seeking to unite young Christians of different
churches and nations in a fellowship of evangelism and
service. One of the continental pioneers of the YMCA,
Henri Dunant (also founder of the Red Cross), writing a
circular letter from Switzerland to other YMCAs, spoke of
the movement as 'an attempt to propagate that ecumenical
spirit which transcends nationality and language, denomi-

Clergy are experts in theology. This gives
false picture of Church to outsiders.
Good for ministers to have seen something of the world
Ministry & laymen are co-workers.
Celibate ministry not advocated.
All work an offering of worship. Task of a
minister is to prepare his people to the Church at
their work.

_____

Miss Horton (St Agnes).
Laity also ministers of God.
Why not visit other churches voluntarily.
Should not all preachers be ordained,

INTER-DENOMINATIONAL BIBLE STUDY
HOUSE MEETINGS FOR OCTOBER

Tue.17: Young People's Bible Study
at 302 Selby Rd.

* * *

Mon 23 :
At 10 Temple Court

Tue 24.
At 71 Coronation Parade

Thu 26.
At 41 Selby Rd.

Fri 27.
At 302 Selby Rd.
Come to one of these House Meetings and
if you can, bring a copy of the New English
New Testament.

nations and ecclesiastical questions ... to realize as much as possible the article of the Creed: "I believe in the Communion of Saints and the Holy Universal Church" '. Thus it was a layman who first struck the note not just of fellowship between Christians, but of this fellowship having the further goal, however remote and dimly seen, of 'realizing as far as possible ... the Holy Universal Church'. At Paris in 1855 the World Alliance of YMCAs was founded. Its basis, with slight alterations, was accepted as the basis of the World Council of Churches at its First Assembly at Amsterdam in 1948.

These lay movements, the YMCA and (founded ten years later) the YWCA, were in a real, though incomplete, sense the pioneers of the ecumenical movement of this century. Through them tens of thousands of young men and women found a Christian fellowship which transcended denominational barriers, which did things that official churches could not do to meet their needs as migrants to great cities, young workers, or students in universities and colleges. One can say of these movements that, for the first eighty years or so of their existence, they left the churches where they were in their relationship to one another; that their ethos was undenominational rather than inter-denominational—and this, by and large, was what the churches wanted them to be. The great service of these lay movements to the later ecumenical movement was that spreading across the world as they did, largely by voluntary lay endeavours, they brought under their influence many young men and women not just as recipients of services, but as active, responsible participants. Thus they gave back to the churches many mature experienced young men and women who became leaders in the churches, both clerical and lay. They did more than any other agency to make members and leaders of 'younger' churches on the mission field and 'older' churches of the West known to one another.

Two Laymen: Mott and Oldham

This chapter is about the contribution of the ecumenical movement to understanding our lay situation and vocation today. This derives not from some particular conference or report, committee or group, but from the whole development of the ecumenical movement and the way in which it has influenced the thinking and the activities of churches over the past fifty years. There is no risk of denial in saying that the movement never could have developed as it did and when it did but for two laymen, John R. Mott and J. H. Oldham. Nor is it just an accident that they were laymen: one cannot say with truth that they might just as well have been clergy. Both were loyal churchmen: neither made any secret or belittlement of this fact. Mott (the elder by ten years) was an American Methodist, Oldham a Scottish Presbyterian and, from the time in middle life when London became his base of operations, an Anglican. As laymen—especially in the conditions of inter-church relations prevailing between 1895 and the first world war—they were far more free to take initiatives which did not commit their churches than any ordained minister of any church could have been. Mr Mott and Mr Oldham calling on Archbishops and Metropolitans did not 'represent' in their status anything but themselves as persons and, later, the organizations they had helped to create and were serving.

But—and it is a 'but' of mammoth proportions—what made Mott and Oldham what they were, and the ecumenical movement proper different from its precursors in the lay movements, was that they used both the freedom and the limitations of their lay status. They could erect platforms, but they could not say on them a single word which carried authority with the churches. That could only be done by the recognized leaders of the churches, and only such spokesmen (and not the individual enthusiast) could carry weight within their own churches. Nor could Mott and Oldham and others have done what they did to bring the ecclesiastical leadership of the churches into new relationships and to the support of new or enlarged causes, if they had not had to hand an actual visible demonstration of a break with 'undenominationalism' in the name of something entirely new—co-operation without compromise of essential doctrinal and ecclesiastical position.

John R. Mott[1] was a first year student at Cornell University when J. E. K. Studd, a member of the famous 'Cambridge Seven', visited it on a mission in 1885-6. As a result Mott—an outstanding scholar—made up his mind to devote his life (in his own words) 'to the service of Jesus'. Later he signed the Princeton declaration, the forerunner of the pledge of the student volunteer missionary union, committing himself, 'God permitting, to go to the unevangelized portions of the world'. In the space marked 'chosen field' Mott wrote 'the world'. There was neither indecision nor facetiousness in this. From the first Mott was inspired by the world dimension of the Christian mission. In rapid and overlapping succession he was secretary for the collegiate work of the YMCA in America, a large movement of extremely rapid growth, chairman of

[1] Many readers will know most or all of what immediately follows: but I am writing for those who do not, and especially for a young layman who took a book out of his pocket and said to me: 'I picked this up on a bookstall—I've never heard of the chap, but he seems to be saying all the things about laity and the Church in the world that I thought were new. Have you heard of him? Name of Mott.'

the kindred but separate Student Volunteer Movement, and (in 1890) secretary of the international student YMCA. This last appointment launched Mott on his career of international travel and took him not only among protestants and evangelicals, but to places where the 'student Y' had already penetrated—among Roman Catholic students in South America and Orthodox students in Russia. He combined in a remarkable way active evangelism among students with organization of continuing work, selecting and sending as YMCA secretaries to India, China and elsewhere some of the ablest men to be found anywhere in the service of the churches.

By 1895 Mott, with his now large experience of students, could convince others of the need he saw. There must be a world-wide federation of students embracing both the 'student Y's' and (as they had developed in other countries) the Student Christian Movements. The World's Student Christian Federation was founded in 1895: it was not to be (as the Evangelical Alliance was) a fellowship of like-minded individuals, but a federation of autonomous national movements of very different stamps. Its general secretary was to be John R. Mott.

J. H. Oldham enters the story as a Scottish student in Oxford, touched as Mott was by the evangelism of Dwight L. Moody and the missionary fervour of the student volunteers. Out of these same impulses had come the Student Christian Movement in Britain, and Oldham at twenty-two became its first general secretary in 1896. 'This meant', he said, 'that having dealt with the correspondence in my own hand I stamped the letters and walked round to Aldersgate Street Post Office and dropped them in the letter box.' But he did far more than organize branches and conferences; he developed a fruitful programme of study and then, taking up his commitment

to missionary work, he departed to India to work with the
YMCA in the university of Lahore. Here he developed
his rare gift, so powerfully used later, for 'spotting' young
men with gifts of mind and spirit and bringing them into
a fellowship which made them think more widely and
deeply and commit themselves more thoroughly as Christians and churchmen, no matter what their subsequent
careers. Typhoid cut short this work and sent Oldham
back to Scotland. He went to New College, Edinburgh, to
read theology, and then to Germany for study. Both his
former posts had been within the range of Mott's own
work as secretary of the WSCF and when he took up work
as the missionary study secretary of his church Mott did
not altogether lose sight of him.

Two things about the Federation made it different from
the lay movements that gave it birth. It was interested in
theology (it had, of course, a number of theological students in its constituent movements): and it took the question of the Church with a new and different seriousness.
These two factors led to a different basis of co-operation
from most of the lay movements. Those who came together brought all their convictions and churchmanship
with them and then wrestled with the problems that the
interplay created. The churches were far from ready for
this—though many of their outstanding figures, especially
their theologians, came regularly to the summer camps of
the SCM as much to meet one another informally and
freely as to join in the lively discussion and high jinks of
the students.

The brevity of student life contributed to a friendlier eye
from church authority. J. H. Oldham tells of visiting
Bishop Charles Gore, of Oxford, the recognized leader of
the Anglo-Catholic wing of the Church of England, and
describing his plans for the movement's programme, in the

hope of getting Gore's support. 'What are you planning to do with these students when they have gone down from the universities?' Gore asked. 'Nothing', was the reply. 'That was what I hoped you would say,' said Gore, 'and on that basis you have my support.'

Others besides Gore would have been unwilling to give their support to a movement which by providing life-long possibilities of fellowship might unintentionally draw young people away from their churches. Great discussions went on also within the Society of the Sacred Mission at Kelham as to whether members of the Society and its theological students should take part in the annual conferences of the SCM (held in those days at Baslow in Derbyshire). Once committed (and the Society took the trouble to print a statement of its reasons for participating) the Society became a warm and sometimes critical friend of the SCM, and Father Kelly in his monk's robes and with his eliptical, tantalizing, challenging speech a familiar and increasingly venerated figure at a long succession of annual 'Swanwicks'.

By such decisions and steps as these was the Anglo-Catholic or High Anglican participation achieved. Anglo-Catholics brought views on Church and sacraments not shared by others and they also found in Baptists and Methodists, Congregationalists and Presbyterians gifts of piety and fellowship, theological seriousness and Biblical understanding and, in some, a churchmanship as 'High' as their own.

Meanwhile Mott was doing work, through the WSCF, which contributed much to ensuring the future participation of the Orthodox in the ecumenical movement. Well known in universities throughout Europe and America, and spending long periods in India, China and other parts of Asia, he yet contrived to give time to understand and see the vital importance of the totally different world of Orthodox Christianity in Eastern Europe, the middle East, and India. To many evangelicals Orthodoxy was a dead or dying relic of the past, a proper field of 'mission'. But this was not Mott's view. To help the Orthodox to make their unique contribution to the whole, to respond to the wide ecumenical vision of the Ecumenical Patriarch, the spiritual head of a large segment of Orthodoxy, was Mott's endeavour.

It was typical of his range and grasp that as a sidesweep to his main work he should find the money to help the impoverished and very important Orthodox seminary at Halki near Constantinople to its feet, or that he should sit down with young students and priests to study the Bible—so that one old priest in Athens could tell me of his parish where 'we always study the Bible together—a thing unthought of in Greece till Mott came'. At Constantinople, in 1911, a great international conference of students organized by Mott crowned the work of several years. The Orthodox were 'in', never to leave, and with them the certainty that 'undenominationalism' was dead. The search for the *oikumene* of the whole Church, which is fire in the bones of the Orthodox, was brought into relationship with the *oikumene* of the Church's mission in the whole world, so passionately served by those who had been influenced by the missionary movement and the evangelical revival.

Edinburgh 1910

The full partnership of Mott and Oldham began in 1908 when by what looked like the accident of illness Oldham was brought to the meeting of the preparatory committee for the World Missionary Conference at Edinburgh in 1910, and before the end was appointed full-time secretary. Mott (as chairman of the preparatory study commissions—a new concept) had already sought Oldham's assistance in shaping the conference. It was not to be a large missionary demonstration organized by, and mainly for, the missionary supporters in one country with delegations from elsewhere. Rather, it was to be 'a conference for study and counsel' on the critical issues facing the missionary outreach of the churches.

It is tempting to tell again the story of the staggering spiritual and organizational achievement of Edinburgh 1910. It was not by any manner of means a conference of missionaries and mission enthusiasts: the churches' leaders were there to discuss the Church's mission. Though the constituent bodies were missionary societies, the personalities were leading churchmen. (The Archbishops of Canterbury and York, and seven diocesan bishops, and the Moderators and Presidents of all the main churches in the British Isles were present as delegates appointed by the British organizing executive.) The organizers provided factual material collected on a vast scale and presented by commission chairmen who had worked at the preparation in the commissions for nearly two years.

Archbishop Randall Davidson addressed the conference: never before had an Archbishop addressed in public an audience containing many members of other churches. He could not have been present had not the SPG rescinded its refusal to attend, largely as the result of Gore's influence. For Gore, knowing something of the SCM, wrote to the SPG that the proposed conference was not on the undenominational basis to which he and they alike objected, but on a new basis which meant no compromise of essential principle. Nevertheless, it was Gore who insisted that, alike in the main sessions and the commissions (one of which he chaired with great distinction), 'doctrine or church polity' should not be discussed.

This limitation led to an incident which was to have totally unforeseen results. Closing an address to the conference on medieval missions and their significance for the present, Frere, the Father Superior of Mirfield, used the words: '. . . Medieval missions have to teach us very much of the power of faith. Let us close our meeting, therefore, with the prayer that the Lord will increase our faith.' Thus far the printed record: but Father Frere as he closed his address raised his arms and prayed: 'O Lord Jesus Christ, who didst say to thine Apostles, Peace I leave with you, my peace I give unto you: Regard not our sins but the faith of thy Church, and grant it that peace and unity which is agreeable to thy will.'

Few can have recognized the context of the prayer as the Roman Missal, but the meaning was clear to many, and to Bishop Brent, Anglican Bishop in the Philippines, it meant a determination to work to bring church leaders together to discuss just those things that Edinburgh had perforce omitted. Returning to the United States he persuaded the Protestant Episcopal Church to support a move to hold a world conference on faith and order. Between the idea and its achievement in 1927 much of the work of persuasion and clarification fell to yet another layman, an episcopalian lawyer in New York, named Robert Gardiner.

From Edinburgh to Jerusalem

An 'Edinburgh continuation committee' was mooted from early in the conference and decided on at the end. The insistence of the Germans that no other full-time secretary would be acceptable to them overruled Oldham's hesitations. Mott, whose chairmanship of the Edinburgh conference had contributed in great measure to its success, was chairman. Soon the first world war broke out: many European missions were then in enemy or debatable territory, and the greatest achievement of Oldham's work was their rescue, almost intact, from the warring, and then from the victorious, powers. This brought him into continuous contact with governments—but these contacts would have been useless without the joint backing of the societies. The forging of an instrument which gave governments the opportunity of dealing, on an increasing number of important issues, with one rather than a dozen bodies changed, over the years, the attitude of some governments to missions, in important ways—not least in giving them a respect for a Christian body that could on a number of issues very firmly resist them.

For a large part of the period after post-war recovery, the main work was to build an effective organ of co-oper-ation. The continuation committee was dissolved, the International Missionary Council took its place. Oldham was joined by other colleagues and was asked to turn his own energies mainly to education. The total stake of all the world's missionary societies in education, from pri-mary school to university, was fabulous. Like most pio-neer enterprises this educational venture helped to create further demands—and these could not be fulfilled. The question of the future policy of missions and their rela-tions to governments became a major issue. Oldham be-came more and more involved with Africa where the needs were so great and the resources so poor. One offshoot of the Council's work was the founding of the International Institute of African Languages and Cultures (1926), to which all governments made contributions. Lord Hailey became its first chairman and Malinowski, the distin-guished anthropologist, one of Oldham's close collabo-rators in this and other ventures.

For our purposes in this book the most important fea-ture of this period is the way in which the IMC—then the *only* world-wide co-operative organization between the churches—pursued the opportunities afforded by the strength of acting together. At significant points they were ahead of governments in thinking about the needs of new nations and the responsibilities of governments towards them. Their officers, and especially Oldham, knew the key men in many spheres—many of whom were, of course, Christian laymen.[1] The chief concern of the Council was with mission policy in an age of accelerating change, and they called on the advice and co-operation of Christian laymen, and indeed of anybody able and willing to help. Statesmen, economists, sociologists, high officials in the International Labour Office, industrialists and trade unionists, were all brought in to advise. When the IMC opposed government policies or inertia they knew the facts, and in taking action were extremely well informed.

In 1928 the IMC held at Jerusalem one of its most important Council meetings. Education was a major topic of mission policy—the provision of general education and religious education. A decision was taken to create a department of social and industrial research. The chief topic, however, was to be 'the Christian Message', to be considered in contrast with other religions. All the subjects were prepared for by the writing of papers and by regional study. Among the papers was one by Rufus Jones, American Quaker, on 'Secularism' and its challenge to Christian faith. It was not presented to the full conference, but to the special meeting devised for its discussion, to which most of the conference flocked. What Rufus Jones had said was elaborated and reinforced by such men as Charles Raven, Canon Oliver Quick, R. H. Tawney

[1] Those who want a detailed account of one aspect of this work will find it in Vol. II of Miss Margery Perham's life of Lord Lugard.

and many others. What use was it for Christian missionaries to bend their energies to refuting the errors of ancient religions and proclaiming the supremacy of the Gospel, while they disregarded the growth of an attitude of
mind deriving from the West and spreading rapidly over
Asia, which centred men's thought in this world (as the
chosen name implied) and on the possibilities of the
achievement of human satisfaction without relation to any
divine order?

Nobody was more forcibly struck by these issues than
Oldham,[1] and for a period after the Council meeting he
devoted a large part of his intellectual energies to reading
and thinking round the vast range of problems opened up.
Edinburgh 1910 had after its title the words 'To consider
missionary problems in relation to the non-Christian
world'. One of its Commissions was called 'Unoccupied
fields'. The assumption of every speaker was the unques-
tioned presence of a secure base for Christianity in the
West, and the presence 'over there' of a large field of operations for mission, a field mainly occupied by other religions. That picture of a mission conceived in terms of
geographical expansion, seen after Jerusalem, seemed to
be standing on its head. If what had been said was true,
then the greatest challenges to Christianity were emerging
in the West. There *was* no 'base' any more, except in the
Church itself and in the Church *everywhere*.

The New Christian Adventure

Jerusalem left a tangled and in some ways embittered
situation concerning the nature of the Christian message.
There were two sharply divided camps: on the one hand

---

[1] Although he was not actually present at Jerusalem, being released
by the Council to take his place on the Hilton Young Commission
on the future of the East African territories.

those (including Mott and most of the Anglo-Saxons) who saw in other religions much that a Christian might retain; on the other hand those who saw a radical and complete break between Christianity and any other religion, including H. Kraemer and almost all the Germans and Scandinavians. The drafting of the statement on the message fell mostly to William Temple and this, centring on the pivotal assertion 'Our message is Jesus Christ', won complete assent. But afterwards the breaches opened even more widely. In the background, not present at Jerusalem, was the giant figure of Karl Barth declaring the otherness of God and the complete inability of man to find him except by his own self-revelation.

A year after the Jerusalem meeting Oldham produced a small pamphlet called *The New Christian Adventure*. It was written in the first place as an appeal to the International Missionary Council, but had a wide circulation and evoked much interest. The gist of it was to point out in clear terms the fact of an emerging world-wide civilization based on science and technology. He carefully did not identify science or technology with secularism, but showed the impetus they gave to belief in man's power to transform and control his world. This would be the world of the rising generation. Who among Christian theologians and leaders would devote himself to the questions being raised for theology, and how could scientists and philosophers be brought to address themselves to the task of helping to bridge the widening gulf between characteristically religious and characteristically scientific ways of thought?

The Jerusalem statement on the Christian message was very widely propagated and discussed. Few conferences have ever been better served by their popularizers. Basil Mathews' *Roads to the City of God* became a study book in thousands of local churches and student groups. The study of 'secularism' was pursued by groups of scholars. The preparatory statement on which they worked was written by Emil Brunner, whose book on *The Divine Imperative* became a classic study of Christian engagement in the secular world, in Europe, Great Britain and America. In Britain, Principals of theological colleges, Anglican and Free Church, were called together, for the first time, by William Paton, to discuss the content of the Christian message in the modern world.

To sum up: mission was no longer to geographical areas of the world: it must be to a culture becoming world-wide. 'World' began to assume a new meaning. 'The Church in the world' meant not only the Church on the map but the Church in a world of men and institutions—political, economic and social—which had become (in the proper sense of the word) 'autonomous', a law to themselves. The era of domination of every area of life by the ecclesiastical institution was long since over, and with it the crippling restriction on human freedom and creativity. From a relationship of domination, the Church passed by successive stages to one of dwindling and often ineffectual contact with large areas of the life of society, especially those areas which were new. This problem had been seen by many outstanding writers and thinkers, but it took the ecumenical movement, with its essential task of understanding anew the doctrine of the Church, to throw into perspective the importance of the laity as the presence of the Church in the secular life of society.

4

THE CALLING OF THE LAITY

'Life and Work'

AMONG the thousands of students to be caught and held by the dawning vision of the whole Church in the whole world, none pursued his early purposes more consistently through a long life than Nathan Söderblom. In his diary during a student conference in 1891 he wrote: 'Lord, give me humility and wisdom to serve the great cause of the free unity of thy Church'. He was present at the world student conference in Constantinople in 1911, and from then on was convinced of the great importance of the Orthodox to ecumenical discussion. As Archbishop of Uppsala and Primate of Sweden during the first world war he worked to bring churchmen together from among neutral and warring nations, with limited visible success. The estrangement and mutual suspicion engendered by the war, even among Christians who had formerly worked together, lasted long after hostilities ended.

Immediately after the war the World Alliance for Promoting Friendship through the Churches (a body with an individual membership founded during the war) met in Holland. Söderblom there proposed a permanent 'Ecumenical Council of Churches'. The proposal was not accepted: it was premature. Nevertheless, he persisted in his efforts to bring about if not a council at least a conference of representatives of the churches, where they would reestablish and develop confidence and turn their attention to their common responsibilities in promoting peace and justice.

In 1925 the First World Conference on the Life and Work of the Churches met. Stockholm was the obvious place and Archbishop Söderblom the obvious chairman. The Orthodox were there in force—their first appearance at a world conference with official representatives of other churches—and made a substantial contribution. Söderblom wrote to the Vatican inviting full participation: his letter was acknowledged with no mention of the invitation. The British, hot from their own successes in organizing the COPEC conference on the churches' action in relation to politics, economics and citizenship, were perhaps the best prepared delegation in the subjects discussed at Stockholm. The Germans came fully back into fellowship. The younger churches were scarcely represented.

As the movement (at first called the Stockholm movement, later the Universal Christian Council for Life and Work) expanded, there were many tensions. There is an idea (one that laymen frequently cherish) that churches and Christians have all their differences in the field of doctrine and order and can 'get down to practical issues together' without much difficulty. This is an illusion. Practical decisions and actions have their spring in attitudes of the mind. What seems plain common sense to a Britisher may seem nonsense to a Greek or a Swiss.

On the whole, churches were more deeply identified with the policies and outlook of their nations then than now. There was no means by which these outlooks could undergo regular mutual correction. Furthermore, many national attitudes owed much of their substance to religion. Lutheranism, Calvinism and Anglicanism had all contributed to national characteristics of temperament and to certain jealously held doctrines, including those of the relation of Church and State. The doctrine of the Two Realms in Germany derived from

Luther's teaching. The doctrine of the separation of Church and State was embodied in the Constitution of the United States. Such differences only came to the surface with attempts to work together. Only as they came out in the open could they be examined anew.

The movement had its headquarters in Geneva. It early set up a study department and took up, in succession, important topics of the day and got them discussed in the individual churches. The Roman Catholic Church had from 1891 its source of authority on social affairs in the great encyclicals which were formative in creating Christian social doctrine. Other churches moved more tentatively: they did not make official pronouncements, and the work of thinking about the Church in society was left to able individuals and unofficial groups, some of which were highly influential. They met in the ecumenical movement.

In 'Life and Work' the disclosure of the sources of disagreement forced the movement ever deeper into the discussion of basic theological issues, including the nature of the Church as the universal divine community. But there was no danger of the movement taking off into the rarefied atmosphere of pure theology. Every biennial meeting of the Council and almost every committee was confronted by some new crisis in the world, and these mounting crises of the '30s all spelled out one theme: the enlarging power of the State in country after country and its increasingly arrogant claims over the minds and consciences of individual men and women.

Oxford 1937

In 1934—long before there was any general realization of the real nature of Nazism among political leaders (or, indeed, among most churchmen)—the Council declared by resolution its support of the Confessing Church in Germany and sent the official delegate of the so-called 'German Christians' back to his Nazi-appointed bishop with what amounted to a stinging rebuke.[1]

The same meeting of the Council decided on the subject matter of its second world conference (Stockholm, 1925, having been the first) to be held at Oxford in 1937. 'The gravity of the modern problem', recorded in minutes circulated to the churches,

> 'lies in the fact that the increasing organization of the life of the community, which is made possible by modern science and technique, and which is required for the control and direction of economic forces, coincides with a growing secularization of the thought and life of mankind . . . No question, therefore, more urgently demands the grave and earnest consideration of Christian people than the relation between the Church, the State and the Community, since on these practical issues is focussed the great and critical debate between the Christian faith and the secular tendencies of our time'.

Archbishop Söderblom died in 1931. He had been a chairman of many parts; above all a man whose vision and faith for the Church were unbounded. It is to him that all of us who take part in the Week of Prayer for Christian Unity owe the articulation of the basis on which we pray. Christ is not divided, and the Church, his Church, is and can be only One. Our prayer is therefore that the Church may become visibly what in truth it is—Christ's one and holy Church.

Söderblom's place was most worthily taken by George Bell, Bishop of Chichester, who chaired the meetings at Fanø described above. His relations with the German

[1] See E. H. Robertson, *Christians against Hitler* (SCM Press, 1962).

Confessing Church were ones of complete trust and inti-
macy: his courage and friendship were to many an un-
shakable spiritual rock in the trials of imprisonment and
later of war.

As chairman, Bell invited Oldham to the 1934 meeting
of the Council at Fanø. He was at once elected chairman
of the Research Department, which was charged with a
three-year task of preparation for the Oxford conference.
Oldham relinquished his long-held position in the IMC
with the complete good will of his colleagues, for this
development was the logical succession to his immediate
pre-occupation with the problems of 'secularism'.

The task of preparation was two-fold. The first object
was to make the churches, in the three-year period of
preparation, aware of the conference and its subject
'Church, Community and State'. Oldham wrote an intro-
ductory pamphlet, 'Church, Community and State: a
World Issue', highly provocative and widely read. Almost
every day something in the newspapers confirmed the
rightness of the choice of theme. The second task was to
plan and carry out the preparation. Three main subjects
were chosen: the Church and its function in society;
Church and community; Church and State. A second
group of subjects related the main conference subject to
the specific areas of education, the economic order and
the world of nations. A third group continued the study of
theological foundations—the Christian understanding of
man; the Kingdom of God and history; the Christian faith
and the common life.

The preparation of the conference material was done by
'editorial teams', each with an outer periphery of some forty
correspondents and advisers. Into this preparation Oldham
and his staff and the main organizers, Dr H. P. van Dusen
and Dr Henry Leiper, for example, in the United

States, and Zankov in the Orthodox world, drew an amazing range and quality of participation not only from theologians but from leading laymen and women in every one of the fields covered by the conference.

Laymen had never before been so widely consulted, or occupied so many places (including the chairmanships of two of the six sections) in any conference of its kind. The conference reports had a stamp of authority as they discussed matters on which it would have been easy to betray an inadequacy of knowledge of the affairs of the world. But the chief note that came out of the conference concerned the Church: 'The primary duty of the Church to the State is to be the Church, namely to witness for God, to preach His Word, to confess the faith before men, to teach both young and old to observe the divine commandments, and to serve the nation and the State by proclaiming the will of God the supreme standard to which all human beings must be subject and all human conduct must conform. These functions of worship, preaching, teaching, and the ministry, the Church cannot renounce whether the State consent or not.' These words were part of the message of the conference.

The influence of Oxford 1937 was widespread, and would have been wider but for the outbreak of the war. It gave another powerful impetus to the process by which men's spiritual sights were being raised from immediate and all-inclusive pre-occupations with their own church in their own nation or community, to the *oikumene*—the whole Church in the whole world. Oxford was a direct step from Jerusalem: Jerusalem identified 'the world' as the world all round the Church, a world of institutions other than the church, decreasingly influenced by the Church, in some senses threatening it by isolating it. Oxford asked: 'How is the Church to make effective contact with this world?' and answered: 'Through the laity who are already there.'

This was clearly put in the preparatory volume for the conference in these words:

> 'In relation to the issues which will come before the Oxford conference nothing could be plainer than that if the Christian faith is in the present and the future to bring about changes, as it has done in the past, in the thoughts, habits, and practices of society, it can only do this through being the living, working faith of multitudes of lay men and women conducting the ordinary affairs of life . . . Obvious as this truth is, and certain as it is to receive assent when stated, it does not, in fact, fill any large place in the picture called up in our minds when we use the word Church. The word does not in the least suggest the work of the world. It suggests Sunday, and what happens on Sunday. We can hardly exaggerate the loss resulting from this restriction of meaning . . .
>
> 'When we speak of the Church fulfilling this or that function in the social sphere, we tend instinctively to think of the clergy doing something about it, or of assemblies in which the clergymen predominate or take the leading part, taking some action. To a far greater extent than we ordinarily realize, our whole thought about the Church has become clericalized. If the Church is to be an effective force in the social and political sphere, our first task is to laicize our thought about it . . . We stand before a great historic task—the task of restoring the lost unity between worship and work.' [1]

---

[1] W. A. Visser 't Hooft and J. H. Oldham, *The Church and its Function in Society* (Allen and Unwin, 1937), p. 117.

1937—1962

As an outcome of the thinking stimulated by Oxford, a number of institutions grew up in different countries in order to explore this role of the laity in the world and to help the laity to operate with Christian understanding. In Germany the 'Evangelical Academies' were born out of the anti-Nazi Confessing Church which had been so strongly supported by some of the leaders of 'Life and Work'. The academies became places where the laity could examine the problems of their life in professions, industry or commerce. They have now built up staff teams of men and women expert in theology, economics, sociology and psychology. Those who attend their courses and confer- ences are by no means all practising Christians: they come to discuss the kind of problems that are pressing on them in industry, trade unions, politics and the profes- sions, and to ask what the Church has to say that will help them where they are. About a hundred 'circles' in different parts of Germany draw together those who, having taken part in an academy course, go on learning. Their closest counterpart in Britain is William Temple College, Rugby.[1]

In Britain the immediate outcome of the Oxford confer- ence was the 'Council on the Christian Faith and the Common Life'. The Archbishop of Canterbury (Lang) was chairman. Its membership, which was deliberately kept small, included the Archbishop of York (Temple), the chief leaders of the Free Churches and an equal num- ber of distinguished laymen, including R. H. Tawney, Sir

[1] A brief account of all the main institutions concerned with lay training for lay activity in the world is to be found in *Signs of Renewal* published by the Laity Department of the World Council of Churches.

Walter Moberly, Sir Fred Clarke, T. S. Eliot and Henry Brooke.

The Council turned its immediate attention to the reform of education in Britain, and its not inconsiderable weight was put behind a memorandum which urged the raising of the school-leaving age, part-time education from school-leaving to the age of eighteen, and the lengthening of the period of training for teachers. Most of these reforms found their way into the 1944 Education Act. But as war was clearly on the horizon, the Council gave its main consideration to the question how to keep alive in the separations of war the conversation between churches about their life in the world so fruitfully engaged at Oxford. It therefore founded the *Christian Newsletter*. Its first number appeared in London three weeks after the outbreak of war, and it continued at first as a weekly and then as a fortnightly for ten years. Oldham's personal acquaintance with most of the leading theologians on the Continent and in America, the catholicity of his own reading and his ability to get busy laymen to give time to the enterprise made the 'C N-L' a meeting place between theology and the life of lay people in the world. Through Geneva [1] the Newsletter circulated in warring Europe, as well as in every part of the allied and neutral world.

The Council on the Christian Faith and the Common Life voluntarily disbanded to pave the way for the creation, in 1942, of the British Council of Churches as the official organ of the churches, and the Christian Frontier Council, composed entirely of lay men and women. Alongside it there continued an older group stemming

---

[1] The study department of Life and Work in Geneva ceased to exist under that name when the two movements of 'Life and Work' and 'Faith and Order' became 'the World Council of Churches in process of formation'.

from Oxford, 'the Moot'. In it theologians, philosophers
and scientists grappled with the intellectual frontier between theology and some of the main lines of thought
issuing from science and the philosophical movements of
the day. The Christian Frontier Council and its sub-
groups turned to intensive study of various fields of Christian lay responsibility. They produced books on the
University, on medicine, on psychiatry, on education, and
fed the *Newsletter* (and its successor *Frontier*) with articles,
including a number concerned with politics, economics and
industry.

All these endeavours in Germany, Scandinavia, Britain
and (to a lesser degree) the United States, carried far and
wide the Oxford concern for a relation between faith and
life which took full account of theology on the one hand,
and expert lay knowledge on the other. But it was mainly
(though not wholly) in relation to the professions—including the newer ones of management and Trade Union
leadership— that the detailed work was done.

When, therefore, the First Assembly of the World
Council of Churches met at Amsterdam in 1948 'The
Laity' was one of the subjects of study asked for by
several member churches. Dr H. Kraemer was the chairman of a commission on 'the laity'. The Assembly's report laid great emphasis on the sociological definition of
the layman as the Christian who earns his living in a
secular calling and not in the service of the Church.

Laymen's conferences were now called together in
Europe and in the United States, and the question of 'The
laity: the Christian in his vocation' was made one of the
six sections of the World Council's Second Assembly, held
at Evanston in 1954. The title was intended, and taken, to
mean both a man's calling as a Christian and his worldly
occupation. The report dealt, as Kraemer later com-

mented, mainly with the Christian in his daily work and not with the structures, organizations and types of personal relationship in which the Christian has to move. The plain fact was that a conference or even a series of them is not enough to explore all that is meant by 'being a Christian in modern society.'

The 1954 Assembly accepted the proposal for a permanent 'Department on the Laity' (emphatically not *of* the laity) designed to study the relevant theological and practical questions and to help the churches with their own thinking. Under the leadership of the Swiss ex-missionary Hans-Ruedi Weber, its full-time director for six years, the department has done just that. Now, far from stimulating churches to take an interest in the question of the laity in the world, it is almost overwhelmed by the demands for assistance in what the churches are themselves doing and planning in the training of lay people for witness and service in the world.[1]

Towards Wholeness

Two chapters have been devoted to an account, mainly in terms of two of its leaders, of the growth and development of the ecumenical movement. Historically this movement was the means by which the vigour and initiative of the Evangelical revival, which poured into the lay and missionary movements of the nineteenth century, turned to meet the Church.

The Evangelical revival and the lay movements came from the churches, divided and disunited as they were. They brought men into a fellowship across the then rigid barriers of denomination. They produced, however, men who were not satisfied to enjoy this fellowship and to

[1] See the department's bulletin, *Laity,* and its book *The Layman in Christian History* (SCM Press, 1963).

leave the churches in their isolation; who coveted it for the churches. Once the historic churches had been afforded the chance to meet (by the early student meetings with their genuine *inter*denominationalism based on regard for conscience, and by the Edinburgh 1910 conference), the inner drive of the Church towards the recovery of that unity which is part of her very being as Christ's Church, began to operate forcibly. It is impossible to believe that, in God's providence, unity can or will stop short of including new relationships on the one hand with the Roman Catholic Church, without which there is no visible *One* Holy Catholic Church, and on the other hand with evangelical movements and groups gathered round the free response of the individual to the Gospel as he hears it. It is impossible to believe that these things can happen without the kind of faith that begins, not ends, with confrontal with an impossible task. We have no right to assume that the unity Christ wills for his Church is going to be fulfilled through the agency of the World Council of Churches as it exists today: we can only offer it to him as an instrument of his purposes and work to make it so. We need some new responsive leap to the action of the Holy Spirit which will carry us on to some new ground where we can meet and understand one another.

Unity means far more than uniting denominations or changing their relationships to one another. A united Church concentrating only on its own life within ecclesiastical frontiers, however widely drawn, is not a *whole* Church in any proper meaning of the word 'whole'. For unless the Church is itself a channel of healing, can it be regarded as itself truly healed? And what, above all, it has to heal, to bring back to unity and wholeness, is the soul of modern man, the man of prolific flowering and no roots.

5

WHO ARE WE?

How Define 'Lay'?

THIS question certainly does not lack answers within the churches. There are plenty of definitions, official and unofficial, of the meaning of 'laity'. But are any of them really satisfactory?

In Roman Catholic Canon Law a layman is one who has not received in addition to baptism the grace of holy orders in priesthood: he is 'one who has no part in the power of jurisdiction and especially of holy order'.[1] But the definition of the laity as 'the non-clergy' is not limited to medieval times or to the Roman Catholic Church: it is widely current today. The *Oxford Dictionary of the Christian Church* (1959) gives under 'laity' the following definition: 'from the Greek *laos,* people. Members of the Christian Churches who do not belong to the clergy.' This is exactly parallel to the usage in the professions of medicine and law, where 'the laity' means those who do not know and may not practise law or medicine.[2]

A learned Belgian Jesuit, Ignatius de la Potterie, has studied the origin of the word 'laic' (singular) and 'laity' (collective). He says that the origin is almost certainly secular, dating back to the time of the Byzantine empire, when so many terms in use in the Church were taken from civil life. If he is right, then the definition of the laity as the 'non-clergy' has a secular origin, and does not come,

[1] Vermeersh and Creusen, *Epitome jus canonicum.* Quoted Congar.
[2] I have even heard a university don say (I trust in an unguarded moment), 'The laity, I mean non-intellectuals ...'

as is so frequently stated, from the Biblical word *laos*.

From being defined as those not possessing clerical status, the laity also came to be defined in the Western Church as those who do not possess the professional knowledge of the clergy, that is to say, a knowledge of theology. This definition also gained strength from the parallelism with medicine and law. (One must remember in this connection that these were the three great professional studies of the medieval university, far closer together then than now.) But in practice lay ignorance of theology is a characteristic of Western Christianity, not of all Christendom.

The Eastern Churches of the Orthodox tradition never regarded the study and teaching of theology as professional monopolies of the clergy. In Greece to this day, candidates for the priesthood are selected by the bishops from among those proposed by a local community from among themselves. The ordinands are trained in pastoral care and more especially in the liturgy, but do not necessarily know any theology at all. Most theological teaching (for example, in the university of Athens) is in the hands of laymen. Most of the theological students are lay men and women destined for teaching in state schools, for evangelistic or pastoral work or simply for an ordinary profession—including government service.

In the West, however, it became even more common after the Reformation than before it that a knowledge of theology should be a monopoly of the clergy and one of the distinguishing differences between clergy and laity. Dr Hendrik Kraemer[1] attributes this to the Reformation stress on preaching. This preaching, which he defines as 'adequate interpretation of the Word of God', required, he points out, 'a specially qualified group of bearers of this

[1] H. Kraemer, *A Theology of the Laity* (Lutterworth Press, 1958), p. 65.

office'. These gradually became the 'theologians', the 'knowers' in the Church, while in society they were acknowledged as the professional representatives of 'spiritual status'. The reservation of preaching to the ordained and theologically trained ministry remains to this day far more characteristic of Lutheranism and the Reformed (Presbyterian) tradition than of Methodism, where the purpose of preaching is conceived not only as exposition, but as witness or testimony, with marked effects on lay participation in preaching.

Behind the difference between the knowers and non-knowers of theology lies another distinction, now no longer existing in fact. Government forms still refer to 'clerks in holy orders'. This is a reminder of the distinction between literate and illiterate. Professor C. N. L. Brooke says:[1] 'Historically clergy and laity have become far more separated than was envisaged in early days, owing largely to the historical accident that in the early middle ages the clergy were literate and the laity illiterate. It is remarkable how much our present traditions still owe to this fact—including the deep anti-clericalism latent in most Englishmen.' He may well be right that some of the tangled relationships between clergy and laity owe more to the past than we know or can acknowledge.

Another definition of the laity is a sociological one: those who earn their living in a secular occupation and not in the service of the Church. As we have seen, this is how 'the laity' was defined at the first two Assemblies of the World Council of Churches. But the definition deserves thought. Definitions, although they do not matter in themselves, may describe and help to maintain attitudes which prevent us from seeing facts or thinking in fresh ways.

[1] In a letter. See his contribution to the symposium *The Layman in Christian History* (SCM Press, 1963).

This is why definitions must be explored, although the exercise may seem wearisome and unnecessary.

To accept a sociological definition of 'laity' is at once a corrective and a capitulation. It is a corrective because it reminds us how often it is just this person who earns his living in the world who is absent from those places and bodies where 'the laity' are said to be present and where the laity in this sense are being discussed. I remember how, at the Amsterdam WCC Assembly, an American layman asked for a show of hands of the laity present in the section on 'God's Design and Man's Disorder'. About one third of the total of 120 responded. But when those who worked for the Church as officials or in the church press were asked to withdraw, only a dozen hands remained raised in a company of 120, all official delegates of member churches of the World Council of Churches. Of the present number of laity in the Church Assembly of the Church of England, totalling 346, 101 are women, of whom 35 are the wives of clergymen; approximately 50 are paid church officials in dioceses or parishes and 14 are employed in church institutions: about 60 are retired from active work. To define laity sociologically as those who earn their living in a worldly occupation is therefore a useful corrective. But if it is used as a substantive definition of laity, then its use marks a capitulation to non-theological terms and the abandonment of the attempt to define laity positively and theologically.

Roman Canon Law also recognized a clear distinction between those who retired from the world, to monastery, nunnery or hermit cell (who might still be unordained), and those who were embedded in the world not only through trade or occupation, but through sex, marriage and family. These were the laity. From the Fathers onwards, the inferior spiritual and moral achievement possible for the laity is a subject of comparison with the true and only possibilities of a holy, dedicated life away from the world and its contaminations and distractions. It is easy to comment on the insufferable supposition that the laity were, just because they were laity, second-class citizens of the Kingdom of Heaven, but less easy to see that the dilemma it attempts to come to terms with is not exclusively a medieval one: it is timeless and universal. How can the radical demands of the Gospel be fulfilled without a deliberate refusal to be the object of conflicting claims on time and money, loyalty and affections? Perhaps our revulsion from the asperity of the Fathers has in it not only our enhanced sense of the possibilities and value of lay Christian life, but also an impaired and diminished sense of the awfulness of God's own perfection and the magnitude of his claim for holiness in those who serve him.

The single greatest general objection to existing definitions of 'laity', and to the attitudes still prevailing which derive from past definitions, is that they are all negative: they say what the laity are not. Furthermore, all these negative definitions have in them a strong element of 'over-againstness' towards the clergy—the clergy are, and the laity are not; the clergy do, and the laity must not. Nobody wants to be an 'is-not': nobody is going to be stirred to response by being told that such is his being and his vocation. And as for this 'over-againstness': who would seriously doubt that in so far as superiority on one side and resentment on the other arose from the acquisition by the clergy at one time of status, power and a monopoly of learning in society, all justification for it has vanished in the present day? Are not the present times far too serious for the Church for her to retain within herself any attitude of 'over-againstness' between clergy and laity, and the crippling inner disunity to which it gives rise?

We shall have to examine in more detail later the Roman
Catholic doctrine of the Church as hierarchy and the
Church as fellowship. On this view, briefly stated, the
Church is first the clergy and what the clergy do as ministers of word and sacraments and guardians and teachers of
doctrine. This constitutes the Church as institution. The
Church as fellowship, recognized though it is as the ultimate reality of the Church, is formed by the institution
and is dependent on it for its existence. Protestantism was
not only a protest against abuses, but a protest against this
basic doctrine which, in fact, only hardened rigidly within
Roman Catholicism after and in response to the Reformation. But even where the doctrine of the Church as antecedently the clergy is rejected in principle, it prevails
widely in practice. Such non-theological factors as the fact
that all clergy and ministers of all major denominations
receive what amounts to professional training (in which
there is a large amount of common content) tends to make
the clergy a profession in the modern sense. The State, the
law, and the community in very many ways lump all
priests, clergy and ministers of religion together as a profession. In modern society the clergy, whatever their
denomination, have become (not, for the most part, by
their own seeking) the 'organization men' of church
plants, including buildings and organized activities. They
have much in common with one another. But as organization men they are at a very great disadvantage compared
with all the rest of the 'managers' in this age of 'the
managerial revolution' in that they are the only full-timers
in their 'plants'. Thus the sociological pressure is towards
putting on the clergy, in virtue of their being the only full-
timers, the main responsibility for running the plant. Thus
it comes about that because we seldom think deeply enough
about what functions belong to the clergy because of their

ordination, and what functions have come to them as the churches' full-time officers, *in practice* the Church is widely regarded by those outside or on the fringe, and to a very considerable extent among the faithful, as primarily 'what the clergy do'. This might be denied: but all kinds of familiar phrases betray what is really the attitude. If an Englishman does not like the vicar he is likely to say: 'Well, let him get on with it: it's his show': if, on the other hand, he approves what the vicar is doing, he talks of 'backing up the vicar', or 'supporting him in his work'. This is not uniquely an Anglican matter: any congregation is likely to expect that a minister will take the lead in building up and sustaining a congregation and a programme of activities. In all churches lay men (and sometimes women) are asked to perform certain duties because there is a shortage of clergy. The reason for giving a more active role to a few lay people is sociological. Although it is often justified theologically, it does not necessarily have any effect on our thinking about the *whole* of the laity—which is the real issue.

One more curiosity in the use of 'laity' must be pointed out before turning to the new search for a positive and theological definition. It is noticeable that a great deal of talking and writing about the laity contains the unexamined assumption that the Church is *other than* the laity with the clergy. In the theological sense, of course, it is: Christ constitutes his Church which is an eternal as well as a historical reality. But even (or one might without exaggeration say 'especially') when matters of church organization, government and finance are being discussed, such titles as 'the position of the laity in the Church' or 'the role of the laity in the Church' are used. Are not such phrases, to say the least, a curious use of language? How can one speak of the laity *in* the Church when they form

99.5 % *of* the Church? One can explain the phenomenon
in various ways, and it is worth commenting on because of
its frequency. Sometimes what is meant is 'key laymen' or
'representative laymen', i.e. office bearers. Sometimes
what is meant is the keen minority or, in some contexts,
'the educated few'. Often 'in the Church' means 'in the
government of the Church'. To be continually telling the
laity that they are '*in* the Church' is to make it more difficult to convince them that they *are,* with the clergy, the
Church.

6

THE PEOPLE OF GOD

'Laos' in the Bible

THE theological attempt to define 'laity' in a positive sense rather than a negative one starts with a re-examination of the Greek word *laos*, people. A few minutes' work will show that none of the uses of the word *laos* in the New Testament conforms at all to the meanings widely accepted today and for so long past, and described in chapter 5.

The word *laos* in the New Testament is used in two ways. It is used, especially in St Luke's Gospel, in a general sense to mean 'men, women and children'—those who heard the Lord preaching, for example, and witnessed the works of healing, and those who listened to the apostles teaching. Often *laos* seems to mean no more than *ochlos,* crowd. *Ochlos* is used in all four gospels of those who partook of the loaves and fishes blessed by the Lord and distributed by the disciples.

But there are also very frequent references in the New Testament to the people of Israel as God's chosen people. Not only are Old Testament passages quoted, but in the Christian preaching and apologetic of the Acts of the Apostles and the Epistles of St Paul the starting place of the whole argument is almost always Israel's particular calling as the *laos tou theou,* the people of God. We are therefore driven back to the Old Testament.

When the Old Testament speaks of 'the nations it means the Gentiles. In the primitive stage of Hebrew religion the early Israelites thought of the Lord, Yahweh, as their tribal god and recognized that other tribes had other gods often associated with an actual territory. But as Yahweh revealed himself to them as the God of all the earth, other gods were seen to be false. The result was two-fold. The hearts of the great religious teachers—prophets, psalmists and lawgivers alike—longed for the time when all men would come to know the God of all the earth and worship him. But to the average good Jew, the gods of the heathen were no gods, their worship was detestable idolatry and their practices morally contemptible. The Jews' despising of their neighbours, however, was mitigated by the generous treatment of strangers enjoined by the Law.

From an early date in Israel's history the word 'people' steadily increased in use, while 'nation' declined except in reference to other nations. Indeed, the nations are spoken of as 'nations but no people' (for example, in Deut. 32.21). The word 'people' is always used collectively and this remains a dominant note even when it is recognized that God does not demand corporate responsibility for all individual guilt (Ezek. 18).

This theme of the people who are made a people by God's call runs throughout the Old Testament. He is committed to them, and they to him, by a covenant or binding promise never broken on his side. In poetic imagery God's people is spoken of in the Bible as *the vine* he tends and from which he expects fruit, as *the beloved child* whose steps the father guides, as *the flock* to whom he is shepherd, as the great and strong *tree* whose roots are by an unfailing river of water, as *the bride* tenderly sought.

All these images, and many more, are applied to God's people Israel as such, and not to part of it. There is no suggestion that God makes his promises or reveals his will to priests as such, or to prophets for themselves. All God's concern is with 'my people'. There is no hint of an idea that the people of God are 'Israel minus the priests'—which would be the Old Testament counterpart of Thomas Arnold's 'What is the laity? The Church!—minus the clergy'. The priests in Israel, in all their set-apartness, their choice from a single tribe, their unique privileges of access to the holy places of Israel's worship, are frequently referred to as 'priests of the people' (just as are 'rulers of the people', 'princes of the people'). In spite of changes which gradually made them more like a caste, the emphasis was on their coming out from among, rather than being over against, all the rest of Israel. And as one watches an Orthodox priest today in rural Greece, his black robe tucked round his waist and the sweat standing out on his face as he smites the stony earth of his fields with a mattock, one can imagine perhaps what the life of Jeremiah's father might have been like at rural Anathoth, or Zechariah leaving his wife Elizabeth and going up to the temple at Jerusalem to do his turn of duty.

The New Testament, where it speaks of the Church as the new Israel or as called by God to be his people, preserves this corporate wholeness. This has nothing to do with the 'collectivity' of the modern world, when men as isolated individuals, unrelated to one another by bonds of community, come together to assert their will in collective power or submit themselves to leaders or ideologies. Israel is called to be a *holy* people, and this means not a collectivity of individual holy men, but a community whose internal and external relations are governed by response to God's demand. The image of the bride for whose life Christ dies that he may present her *spotless* before God, is only one of the images taken from the Old Testament imagery of God's dealings with Israel and applied to the Church.

This will all need further examination in a different context later. The point now is that any effort to show that 'laity = *laos* = people of God' breaks down completely. The Bishop of Southwell's strictures on those who think they have explained something by producing the Greek for it are entirely justified at this point. Has the exploration of *laos* therefore produced a dead end? Yes: but also a new beginning. Nothing said in the Bible about the people of God can be claimed exclusively for what we commonly call 'the laity': but a new field of theological insight opens up when we begin to reflect on what it could mean that the Church is 'the people of God'. This exploration quickly becomes more than an academic study. It can illuminate our practical experience of the Church in the world today: and this is happening.

The conclusion we are reaching is that there is no such thing as a theology of the laity alone, but that there is the possibility of a real shift of emphasis in the doctrine of the Church. Supposing it could be that the word 'laity', instead of calling at once to mind the 99.5 % of church members who are not ordained, made one think of the essential people-like character of the Church of God? As one uses 'unity', not to mean anything organizational or structural but to express the existing unity of the Church in its one undivided Lord and the earnest and prayerful search for its visible expression, so one ought to see in the use of such a phrase as 'the laity of the Church' a reminder of the people-character of the whole Church. 'A theology of laity' ought not therefore to mean 'a theological interpretation or justification of the existence and functions of the 99.5 % of the Church's membership who are not clergy, monks, paid workers of the Church, etc.' It should mean 'a theology of the whole Church as the people of God'. It should define and describe in understandable theological terms (for a theology *of* the people of God must be *for* the people of God) what it means to see the Church in this aspect, and therefore what God is calling his people to be and do.

It is extremely important not to claim for the 'people-image' of the Church that it is adequate to define every aspect of a full doctrine of the Church. It has to be seen in relation to other definitions and descriptions, deriving equally from the New Testament, and most especially to the concept of the Church as the Body of Christ.

But if a re-affirmation of the 'people-character' of the Church is to do its work as a corrective and as an inspiration, it *must* be taken seriously, theologically speaking. Here one is up against a number of difficulties, including the glib talking about 'laity' going on today in some places. But the chief problem in any theological discussion is that the image of the Church as the Body of Christ has been given in the Roman Catholic Church, and in some other quarters also, a kind of pre-eminence over all other images which carries it beyond the range of being an image. When therefore the two statements 'the Church is the Body of Christ' and 'the Church is the people of God' are made, a different force is given to the word 'is'. Bluntly and extremely put, the first is in certain quarters regarded as a clear statement of fact, the second as a derivative of the first (as Father Congar explicitly states: 'People of God precisely because Body of Christ').[1]

I believe the pre-eminence of the concept of the Body over all other images to be right, but I believe that our present understandings of the meaning of 'the Body of Christ' are in need of correction. Theologians must be

[1] *Lay People in the Church* (Chapman, 1959), p. 22.

asked whether the image of the Body cannot perhaps be
better understood—especially in our day of fierce theological debate about church order—if we allow to other
images a sufficient force and validity for them to correct
some of our present understandings of the meaning of 'the
Body'. The fact that our churches have their strongest
disagreements about orders of ministry has led, in situations where unity is discussed, to major attention being
given to this matter and less to aspects of doctrine of the
Church in which there is already agreement. The ecumenical discussion of the people aspect of the Church is therefore a necessary corrective. But unless eminent theologians
are prepared to devote serious attention to the matter, and
unless their words are listened to with a like seriousness,
it will not be of any profit to the Church.

The New Testament use of the phrase 'people of God'
for the Church must be seen both in relation to the dominant theme of the Old Testament, and in relation to the
other images of the Church which appear in the New
Testament. Our introduction (it can be no more) to a
theological understanding of the meaning of 'the people of
God' must begin, however, by re-emphasizing the interdependence of social facts and human experiences with
theological thinking. This is not easy, especially for lay
people. The New Testament speaks in sublime terms of
the Church, the spotless bride of the Lamb slain for her,
sinless and perfect. It is hard to look round at the Church
as one knows it and not to exclaim, 'What! all *that* about
this collection of people? Impossible!' Knowing something
of the pride and arrogance, the persecuting zeal and intellectual blindness which have stained some of the pages of
church history, one prays for a humble frame of mind in
Christian people; an avoidance of thinking of ourselves or
our church 'more highly than we ought to think'. But if

our knowledge of the sociological situation of the Church in the world is too scanty, we can also say that our vision of the wonder of the Church is too dim. If this or that company of Christians is spoken of as 'the Church' in that place it is so not because its members have contracted together to form a church but because it stands there worshipping, serving the Lord of the Church as part of the one Church of the One Lord, in all places, in all centuries of time and in eternity. Nothing less than this vision is a vision of the Church, and every congregation in it partakes of the nature of the whole.

It is a striking and reassuring fact that the most exalted language in the New Testament about the Church, its nature and calling, comes from the pens not of visionaries in ivory towers, but of exactly those men who knew local congregations intimately. There are in the New Testament, notably in the Epistles and in the book of Revelation, descriptions of the facts of church life which will strike many as very much like the situation they know in their own churches. There are 'not many wise, not many great'. There are some very carnal sins. There is a good deal of bickering and place-seeking. Christians compromise with pagan custom, grow lukewarm, fall away. There is also sacrifice and generosity, persistence against obstacles, patience under trial, devotion to the Lord of the Church, and genuine love of the brethren. As one reads the fulminations of St Paul against moral lapses and lack of faith, it is not always easy to remember the bonds of deep affection which bound him to his readers. Sinful and weak they might often be, but to him they were 'my joy and crown'. On their side it was not fear or even respect, but loving devotion which evoked from the little band of elders visiting him at Miletus the tears and kisses with which they entreated him not to go up to Jerusalem, and the same personal affection filled the hearts of the sorrowing company 'with wives and children' praying on the sands at Tyre and watching the boat carry him away from their sight for ever. We may search the book of Acts and the Epistles for the mystical images of the Church which portray its true and divine origin and nature. We may try out of the slender facts there provided to reconstruct the hierarchical, disciplinary and didactic order of the Church, but in the end we are bound to confess that neither the vision of the mystical being of the Church nor the order implanted and upgrowing in it can be separated out from the men, women and children of actual local churches, whose prayers and worship, whose devotion to their Lord, their leaders and one another made the visible fellowship, and whose sins and shortcomings put such strain upon it.

How could St Paul, St Peter and St John write in the same documents to the same people such devastating castigations of individuals and of whole congregations, and such sublime poetic descriptions of the Church? Were they guilty of double-think, of keeping the realities and the vision in separate compartments? This theory will not stand for a moment: for the passages describing in images the wonder and glory of the Church are embedded in and indeed part of the rebukes and warnings. The key is love, love flowing through these apostles, who are also pastors, missionaries and teachers, to the congregations and their members. Only love can bear the distress of facing the bleak facts in truth and at the same time retain the vision unimpaired. It may be that what our theological discussions of the nature of the Church lack is not learning or wisdom but love of the Church as we experience her, in the name of what she really is.

The Church as Body and as People of God

To turn to the images of the Church in the New Testament is not to leave the realities of our visible churches behind. There are over eighty images of the Church and the Kingdom of God in the New Testament.[1] Most of them are embodied in a single line of teaching and make a single point. Many of these are no more than similes—the wild olive, the salt. No harm would be done to the meaning if the phrases were rendered 'you are like wild olive', 'you are like salt'. With many of the images of the Kingdom appearing in the Gospels it is not possible to say whether they were meant to apply directly to the Church or not. Those that occur in the Epistles do directly refer to the Church; of these the most familiar is the image of the Church as the Body of Christ. It is also the most powerful, linked as it is on the one hand to the crucified and risen body of Christ, the central events of the work of man's salvation, and on the other hand to the *Corpus Christi,* the body received by the faithful in Holy Communion.

The image of the Church as the body of Christ is developed in the New Testament in letters bearing traditionally the name of St Paul. It has three elements: (1) the relation of the body to the Head; (2) the inter-relating functions of the members within the body; and (3) the right ordering of the bodily life of those who are members of Christ's body.

The *first* element, the relation of the body to the Head, is stressed in the Epistles to the Colossians and the Ephesians. In the Epistle to the Colossians the Head is spoken of as the source of nourishment and growth in the body (Col. 2.19). The Epistle to the Ephesians makes the

[1] See Paul Minear, *The Images of the Church in the New Testament* (Lutterworth Press, 1961).

same point but adds that the growth is in love (Eph. 4.9). The symbol of the body and its relation to the head is very close to that of the building or archway, of which Christ is again the head or cornerstone. Unlike the symbol of the head and the body, the symbol of the building or archway finds a place in the very earliest preaching of the apostles, namely in St Peter's announcement that, in the resurrection of Jesus Christ of Nazareth from the dead, 'the stone the builders rejected has become the head of the corner'. The healing of the cripple at the gate of the temple was 'a sign' of this (Acts 4.11).

The same quotation from Psalm 118 is found in Matt. 21.42, following the parable of the vineyard in which the treacherous tenants first beat up the owner's servants and then kill the heir. Here it looks as though pre-occupation with who the next tenants are to be has overlaid somewhat the force of the use of the quotation which is, exactly as in Acts, a reference to the resurrection. The tenants—and the Jews, well-versed in the imagery of themselves as God's vineyard have no difficulty in recognizing that Jesus means them—will kill the Son, but this is not the end: God will see to it that the rejected stone becomes the 'head of the corner'. This the apostles announce: the murdered Son has been raised from the dead. Just as the Epistles to the Colossians and Ephesians speak of the head of the body as the source of the body's life and growth, so in a close parallel the First Epistle of St Peter (2.4) speaks of 'that living stone rejected by man' (again referring to the risen Christ) and of those who 'come to this living stone' as themselves becoming 'living stones built into a spiritual house'.

To sum up: the Head of the Body and the headstone of the corner are parallel symbols of the headship of Christ in his Church. He, the living, risen head, imparts life and enables growth. This growth is described in Ephesians as 'growth up into him who is the head' (Eph. 4.15), while immediately before the passage in I Peter where the symbolism is of living stones, reference is made to 'growing up into salvation' (I Peter 2), using the same Greek phrase. 'Christ is the head of the Church his body and is himself its saviour' (Eph. 5.23). Life and salvation flow from the head, but also back to it in the growth and maturity of the members of the body. There is no difference between the corporate relation of the Church to the head, and that of the individual Christian. There is one source of growth, Christ risen; one object of growth, 'into Christ'. 'Catholic' and 'evangelical' are one.

The Church: a Body with Parts

The *second* element in the symbolism of the Church as the body of Christ is the function and relation of the parts or members. On this aspect of the symbolism controversies have raged which have divided the Church. They have given rise, and are still giving rise, to new groups of Christians who claim to understand the symbolism aright.

Some of the passages in the Epistles are clearly no more than a reminder to Christians that they are all members of Christ's body and must care for, be patient with, and respect one another as such. Other passages speak of gifts of grace (*charismata*) which differ from one member to another but do not necessarily presuppose either regularization into offices or functions or the concentration of one gift in one member to the exclusion of all other gifts (Rom. 12.4-8; I Cor. 12.4-11). Yet other passages speak of the appointing in the body of apostles, prophets, teachers in numbered order, followed by workers of miracles, healers, helpers, administrators, speakers in tongues (I Cor. 12.28-30).

This is the point at which divisions arise: for some Christians the essential matter is the showering of the gifts of grace on the Christian community and their exercise within it. The presence or absence of such gifts is recognized by fruits, not by titles and offices. This applies not only to such bodies as the Society of Friends, but supremely to the Pentecostal churches and sects among whom may be found not only the extravagances of the unbridled exercise of a variety of gifts, but also an immense power of growth by a missionary contagion almost entirely on the part of the laity. Even among these communities there is, in the interests of order, an Order of pastors (albeit not full-time professional clerics). These pastors are highly skilled in channelling the outbreaks of spontaneity. They are teachers of converts, lay officers of the congregation: and the older sects become the more they rely for their continuance on the canalizing of gifts into offices.

The meaning of hierarchy in the Roman Catholic doctrine of the Church is vitally important. In a section headed 'Two aspects of the Church' Father Yves Congar puts the matter thus: 'In her ultimate reality the Church is men's fellowship with God and with one another in Christ. She is also the totality of the means to this fellowship. The very word *ecclesia*, he points out, means 'the convocation or assembly' and, he adds, the fact that it is an assembly created by God's action does not prevent it being made up, as such, of its members. 'The Church, in her ultimate reality' (he uses the phrase more than once), 'is a fellowship of persons'. On the other aspect he says: 'The Church exists antecedently to the faithful to constitute them precisely as their Mother.' [1]

With this last sentiment anyone with a knowledge of the history of the Church would agree. Indeed, it is prac-

[1] *Lay People in the Church*, pp. 22-24.

tical experience that we come to, and are formed by, a Church already there with its worship, sacraments and regular order. But by 'antecedently' neither Congar nor any other Roman Catholic past or present means 'previously in history'. He and they mean the word ontologically. The Church as Mother is a higher *order*, without which the fellowship of persons could not exist.

Congar goes on to describe how the Roman Catholic Church fought back against the excesses deriving from the Protestant emphasis on the Church as 'community of persons in fellowship with God and their fellows' by defining and re-stressing (and, he makes no bones about it, in his view *over*-stressing) the hierarchy. This happened not only in the sixteenth and seventeenth centuries, but received the most clear and authoritative reiteration in the 1917 form of the *Corpus Juris Canonici*. Into this doctrine of hierarchy enters, says Kraemer, all the age-old, deep-dyed sentiment that the clergy represent the sphere of the sacred and the laity that of the world. The laity therefore are, as Congar admits, the *passive* recipients of the actions of the clergy.

However, a characteristic of the laity is that from time to time they erupt as the *active* agents of some new impulse of the Holy Spirit. For his gifts are showered out, and the Spirit 'who spake by the prophets' does also speak by ordinary men and women.

'Catholic Action' is the name given to a number of movements which developed in the Church and were formed into organizations under clerical leadership after the first world war. The original movement of young Catholics in industry ('Jocists') gave rise to others in agriculture and among sailors. The object was to prevent young workers from drifting away and, more positively, to draw them together by a sense of solidarity of com-

mitment to one another and to the Church. Catholic
Action met not negation but encouragement in the highest
quarters of the church. Pope Pius XII addressed the re-
invigorated laity in terms they had never heard before:
'The laity are the Church; they make the Church'. To
Congar, in particular, this looked like an opening door to
a restatement on theological grounds of the meaning of
laity. But such a restatement cannot be added on to a
doctrine of the Church as 'antecedently' the clergy and
what the clergy do, without profoundly disturbing the
present definition of the relationship between the two
aspects of the Church. If such a restatement were thor-
ough-going and serious in intention, then it would cause
not a submersion of the one by the other, but a new
relationship between the two aspects, and their *inter-*
dependence would become more obvious.

The importance of such a development for Christian
unity can hardly be exaggerated. The same events are
pressing on all Christians, whatever their church, and are
leading to a common understanding of the gulf which
separates the Church from the world and divides the
consciousness of the laity into 'churchman' and 'man in
the world'. If the bridging of this gulf depends only on an
active clergy, on the Church as hierarchical institution,
and not in any way on lay initiative, one must indeed
exclaim 'God help the Church'.

One of the speakers at the 1961 New Delhi Assembly
of the World Council of Churches, Dr Nikos Nissiotis,
spoke of 'carrying the spirit of Orthodoxy as a gift to
other churches'. It could indeed be that precisely in this
matter; the Eastern Orthodox Churches have a gift for all
of us, including Roman Catholics. For the Orthodox have
preserved a different kind of relationship between the
hierarchical institution of the Church and the whole

fellowship. For them bishops are indeed the guardians of doctrine, priests the administrators of the sacraments, but all within a far livelier, more immediate awareness of the wholeness of the Church as the redeemed community in which all are active participants.

This has practical results in many ways. There can be, for example, no promulgation of doctrine *ex cathedra*, nor is any ordination valid without the acceptance of the candidate by people and clergy. In part the difference between East and West must be due to history: that for centuries Greek and Syrian Orthodox, Copts and Armenians have lived under Mohammedan rule. In Paris, as I watched representatives of the two catholicates of the Armenian Church received into membership of the World Council of Churches, my mind went back to the tenacious preservation of the life of the Church in the homes of the people over long periods of persecution when no public worship or teaching was possible. The same experience has come to the Russian Church in forty years of Communist rule under which none of the ways of passing the faith from one generation to another have been possible except the celebration of the liturgy in churches constantly being reduced in number, and the teaching and practice of the faith in the homes. It is impossible not to take the laity seriously when the very survival of the Church owes so much to them and when their own training in liturgy and in life prepares them for a more active role.

The Church: a Body of Bodies

We must turn now briefly to the *third* aspect of the imagery of the Bible—the relation of the Church as the Body of Christ to the physical bodies and fleshly life of Christians.

It is an exciting thing to visit Corinth and to see there

the market place with its many temples and altars. In this busy port there must have been an extraordinary mixture of experimental religion where everything could be tried and every sort of sexual licence and aberration. Nobody there would have thought that the one was inconsistent with the other, and it is not surprising that the small Corinthian church gave to St Paul so many causes for saying that belonging to the Body and partaking of the Body and Blood of Christ was not some mystery cult pandering to a taste for religious sensationalism but a radical demand on the believer to change his attitude to his own fleshly body. So it is in his letters written to the Corinthians, and written at Corinth to the Romans, that St Paul talks meaningfully about the body.

Lay people are those who use their bodies and do so, not of choice, but of necessity: life in the world means this. It means life in families, mating and begetting. It means work, done of necessity in order to live and to support one's family. To the Greeks the life of necessity was intolerable, a life only for slaves. Aristotle regarded slavery as self-evidently justified: without it free men could not be free, because they would be compelled to do things without which a household will not run. Christianity, on the contrary, honoured bodily work. It denied that freedom or human dignity or spirituality were inconsistent with physical toil. All could be found within the life lived in the world. The body, even the sexual activity of the body, may be hallowed by the Holy Spirit. If the body is the temple of the Holy Spirit, every part of it and every activity of it is included as part of that temple. Pursuing the metaphor from the temple to what went on in the temple, our bodies are living sacrifices offered to God.

Now the doctrine of the Church as the Body of Christ is often discussed without any reference to this aspect of it. How often is the life of the Christian regarded as an *outcome* of the life of the Church! But these bodily lives are the things that Christ uses to build it up. The 'living stones' which he uses to upbuild the Church are not souls or spirits, but whole persons who are being built up into a salvation (wholeness) which includes their bodies. 'Know ye not that your bodies are members of Christ? . . . Therefore glorify God in your body and in your spirit, which are God's' (I Cor. 6.15,20). The body-imagery of the Church does not therefore refer solely to the inward life of the Church. It reaches out into the life of the world through the body-life of Christians.

At this point it links closely with the image of the Church as the people of God in the world. The Church is a physical presence given in the midst of time and place.

The Church: a New People, a New City

St Paul is very careful *not* to identify the Gentile Church as the replacement of Israel in God's will and plan. He tells Christians at Rome that they are a branch of wild olive grafted into the old stock of an olive tree. They are fed by its roots, and woe betide them if they despise those roots. 'Thou bearest not the roots but the root thee . . . if God spared not the natural branches, take heed lest he also spare not thee' (Rom. 11.18,21). This is not just Paul the Jew, but Paul the Apostle speaking, warning the Church that God will not deal less harshly with them than with Israel, and adding that God has still not finished with Israel. The Gentiles are a means of God's mercy towards his ancient people.

It would therefore be a gross misunderstanding of the image of the Church as the people of God to say that the Church simply replaces Israel whom God has cast off. Everything, literally everything, that the Church is in

Christian thought, derives from Christ. The Church is only the people of God because Christ in his own person fulfilled the covenant which God made with Israel. This is the meaning of the eager searching of the Old Testament that went on in the early Church. They were not looking for parallels between the Church and Israel, but for complete conviction that at every point Christ did fulfil the destiny of Israel laid on her by divine command. The eyes of the two disciples walking to Emmaus are opened when at the end of the journey he takes bread and breaks it before them. But to what are their eyes opened? Not only to the identity of this stranger with the Jesus whom they had seen breaking bread on the night of his betrayal, but to the truth of all he had said to them on the walk, when he showed them out of the scriptures that the Christ, the hope of Israel, had to suffer. This had been said at intervals in the earthly ministry of our Lord, but was never understood.[1] Even at the Ascension the disciples try to tell Jesus that there is one thing left undone that the Christ ought to do, to restore the kingdom to Israel.

By the study of the scriptures the Church identified every part of Israel's life as fulfilled in Christ. He is prophet, priest and king. He is also the sacrificed lamb, he is the temple, in him the law is fulfilled, the covenant kept. In him Israel's mission to the nations to bring them to the City of God is realized.[2]

The Epistle to the Hebrews is a sustained exposition of this fulfilment of Israel's role in Jesus Christ of Nazareth.

---

[1] See T. W. Manson, *The Servant Messiah* (Cambridge, 1953).
[2] Caiaphas, remarking that the escape of the nation from the vengeance of Rome by the death of one man was cheap at the price, was, says St John, prophesying, i.e. seeing deeper into the reality of the matter, for he was saying that this death would do what the nation had not done and bring together all the scattered children of God (John 11.49-52).

It is not a mystical exercise in the juxtaposition of texts. Just as the gospel records frequently refer back from an incident in the life of our Lord to some incident or piece of prophecy in the Old Testament, so this account of the achievement of Israel's mission in Christ is filled with references to the earthly life of Jesus (this is the name most frequently used of him in this Epistle)—to his temptation, the antipathy of the Jews, the agony in the garden (where he, the priest, offered up the cries and tears of himself, the victim), his demeanour in the trial and scourging (accepting what he suffered as obedience), the walk to the place of crucifixion outside the gate and the shameful humiliation of the cross.

Not only the Epistle to the Hebrews, but every part of the New Testament, points to one thing. In the life, death and resurrection of Jesus Christ all that God promised to and demanded of Israel is summed up and achieved. The Church is not a continuation, but a new beginning *after* the achievement, a new creation *by* that achievement. That new beginning does not invalidate the old, which takes on new meaning in the light of its fulfilment. So the law is not abolished, except as a way of achieving salvation: it is put in the context of the 'new commandment' of love. Sacrifice is not abolished, but the one supreme effective sacrifice of himself by the Great High Priest makes the offering of Jewish sacrifices superfluous.

As has already been said, the New Testament applies some of the imagery originally used of Israel to the Church. The number of direct references to the Church as the people of God is small. When Peter, Paul and Barnabas all testify to the council of apostles and elders summoned at Jerusalem that God has been working among the Gentiles through their preaching, James sums the matter up by saying that this is in accordance with the promises of God. He has now fulfilled his word by visiting the Gentiles 'to take out of them a people for his name'. The Gentiles are on several occasions referred to as hearing the word when it has first been preached to the Jews. God's action among them is to turn them from a rabble of sheep going astray (I Peter 2.25), who 'in time past were not a people', into 'the people of God' (I Peter 2.10). What has been promised in the Old Testament is 'a light to lighten the Gentiles'. The coming of the light does not result in a diffused twilight among the Gentiles on the periphery of the people: it has the effect of drawing them towards the light and towards one another, and out of them God makes 'a people for himself'. The New Testament cannot tolerate a notion of 'private Christians'. They belong to God together.

Against the dangers of a divided people of God, Jewish and Gentile, St Paul throws all the force of argument and persuasion. He regards it as intolerable that the reconciling power of Christ should stop short of breaking down the 'middle wall of partition' between Jew and Gentile. He tells the Jews that if they go on keeping the particulars of the Jewish law (especially circumcision, the mark of Jewish nationhood) they are using the law as a sort of insurance policy and have not therefore put their full trust in the Gospel. This is the argument of the Epistle to the Galatians. There is only one people of God.

The first Epistle of St Peter is addressed 'to the strangers scattered throughout Pontus, Galatia, Cappadocia, Asia and Bythinia'. They are undergoing persecution. To these scattered believers in their small, not always harmonious companies, the words: 'Ye are a chosen generation, a royal priesthood, an holy nation, a peculiar people, that ye should shew forth the praises of him who hath called you out of darkness into his marvellous light' are spoken.

'From darkness to light' is the characteristic calling of the Gentiles. Scattered as they are, they are yet made one people by Christ, and as one people they are called to exercise priestly functions of offering praise. They are set apart by God, not from the world, but in the world. They are, says the following verse, 'pilgrims and strangers', just as the Epistle to the Hebrews speaks of Christians as those who have 'no continuing city' but 'seek one to come'. The pilgrim is not like a tramp or a refugee. His relinquishment of ties with one part of the world is for a destination beyond it; his journey through the world is purposive, not aimless, and as he journeys through the world he does not despise it but enters into conversation with all whom he meets.

The city and the search for a city is a moving theme in the Old and New Testaments. Although there are plenty of examples of evil cities (like Sodom and Gomorrah); of cities like Ur which have to be left, by God's call, for a life of wandering in tents; of cities condemned like Babylon and Nineveh; yet the city is the ideal of community. Jerusalem in the life of Israel evokes every emotion of loyalty.

I remember a discussion in which modern cities were being deprecated. A young Indian suddenly entered the conversation: 'You wouldn't feel like that if you lived in the heart of rural India and were young and had some education. The city is the place where you find yourself, where you can make choices, where relationships are free, not dictated.' This was said with a light in the eye that made it convincing as a piece of experience, convicting the rest of us of belonging to an old civilization (the very word comes from the city states) grown tired.

The city is the search of a people for free community and for the achievements for which there is only time and energy when the basic necessities of life can be gained without the exhaustion of every particle of time and energy. This search for the truly free community, and for the right use of man's corporate creativity, is part of what Christians mean when they look for the City of God among men.

The island of Patmos rises steeply out of the Mediterranean to a rocky summit crowned for many centuries by a monastery and a church. It is off the regular tourist routes: it has hardly any roads: the main modes of transport are still the donkey and the mule. The church is deeply scarred by the cracks made by successive earthquakes; but it is still a place of worship. The monastery is a maze of little cells grouped round a tiny courtyard: its library contains some of the most ancient fragments of the text of the New Testament and a handful of monks carry on the long tradition of worship and prayer and study. To the Orthodox the whole company of heaven is a vivid reality in his worship. His worship indeed is offered as a part of theirs. Orthodox Christians, says one writer, 'come to the liturgy as guests to a banquet, at which the saints have the place of honour'. They communicate this awareness at times to others. It is not awareness of the past, but of the eternal present. Looking out from the white-washed parapet of the monastery over the dark blue of the Mediterranean which stretches away in every direction, it is not hard to believe that this is the very spot where the vision of the new heaven and the new earth came to St John.

The New Testament closes with the new city coming down to the new earth, and with the promise that 'the tabernacle of God is with men, and he will dwell with them, and they shall be his people and God himself shall be with them and be their God'.

7

THE PEOPLE OF GOD IN THE WORLD

'Every Foreign Country a Fatherland'

THE New Delhi Assembly of the World Council of
Churches in 1961 was markedly different from previous
ecumenical conferences in many respects, and most of all
for the way in which it brought home to every person
there, and to a vast number of those who followed it with
their prayers and interest, the simple fact that there *is* a
people of God in the whole world. The old geographical
picture of a Christendom in the West with outposts and
dependencies in Asia and Africa had disappeared. There
are churches outside Europe, America and the British
Commonwealth which number many hundreds of thousands, some, several millions. Small and weak the churches
may be in many places, but they are not any longer dependencies. In their relations with one another and in the
quality of their life and leadership and their own growing
commitment to evangelism and to service, they have become initiators. Above all, many of them are tackling the
question of 'being the Church' in nations achieving inde-
pendence, in economies undergoing radical change, in
ancient societies being broken to pieces, with all that that
entails of strain and stress on individuals, families and
communities.

A second new feature at New Delhi was the coming of
the Russian Orthodox Church into membership of the
World Council of Churches. No event at the Assembly
was more widely or extensively reported, though it had

been long prepared. The Orthodox are now the largest confession represented in the World Council of Churches, representing roughly one third of the total membership of member churches. Startling things are happening both within the Orthodox world and in the relationship—long broken and strained—between the Orthodox and other ancient Eastern churches such as the Copts and Armenians. Those who thought of the people of God in the world as the Western tradition plus its missionary expansion are now seeing how much more widely spread and greatly diversified that people really is.

But that is not all. Since New Delhi there have been further applications for membership, accepted at the Paris meeting of the WCC Central Committee in August, 1962, for ratification by the member churches. These include the large Russian Union of Evangelical Christian Baptists, Lutherans in Baltic countries, Orthodox in Georgia, Armenians in Southern Russia. The World Council of Churches has lost from effective membership the churches of China, but in other respects its most substantial recent gains in membership have come from countries under Communist rule.

This people of God lives on both sides of the Iron Curtain. But can it communicate across it? Once inside the fellowship, member churches all experience an enlargement of that fellowship through exchanges of visits, a growing volume of help and stimulus to the life of the churches in such forms as books for libraries, scholarships for theological and other students, visits from one church to another, joint working on common undertakings organized by the World Council of Churches in fields as wide apart (seemingly) as discussion on the early Fathers and international affairs. People who talk about the ecumenical movement as 'globe-trotting' and utter weary sighs at the thought of 'meetings' often have very little idea how churches in isolation long for fellowship. One cannot live for ever on the glorious thought of being one people of God with the whole Church in every age and place and bear cheerfully and creatively the complete lack of any tangible expression of this oneness. To enjoy isolation is to atrophy, and churches which have isolation inflicted on them do not normally enjoy it: they yearn for it to be broken. As water will find its own level through a vast intricacy of channels and barriers, so the Church of God, unless it is thwarted, reaches out towards the Oneness in fellowship which belongs to it by nature of its creation by its One Lord.

Nothing was more exhilarating at New Delhi than the gusto with which the Russians leapt into the conversation. Thus far one may thankfully say that there is a conversation going on between churches who live under every type of political system or ideology to be found in the world. Their relationships to state and society vary greatly: they certainly do not agree about many things. They believe that it is right to bring into the conversation the fact of disagreement, but to put those disagreements into the context of a deep and wide agreement about who and what they are. For such progress has been made that nobody within the fellowship thinks of 'unity' as some abstract 'invisible Church'. Unity has to do with the Church in its historical reality: whatever unity may turn out to be, it must carry our present divided churches out of their divided state into a unity that is visible, of which the initiator is Christ and the portent the Church-as-fellowship which we now experience. But active concern with the world— with the sufferings of the poor and needy; with peace; with problems created by rapid social change; with race tensions and the possibility of overcoming them—these are all present as part of the discussion of what it means to be the one people of God in the world.

What we are seeing happening is a twofold process. There must be *a closer engagement* between a local or regional church and the culture and society in which it is set (from which it was often very sharply withdrawn in the period of missionary expansion), and, on the other hand, there must be *a drawing together* of churches out of many cultures and national and ideological situations into a more acute awareness of belonging to a people of God which lives in the world but is not of it.

We seem to be coming back somewhat to the situation described in the letter of an anonymous writer to an otherwise unknown recipient 'Diognetus' in the second century AD.

> 'For Christians are not distinguished from the rest of the world either in locality or in speech or in customs. For they dwell not somewhere in cities of their own, neither do they use some different language, nor practise an extraordinary kind of life. Nor do they possess any invention discovered by any intelligence or study of ingenious men, nor are they masters of any human dogma, as some are. But while they dwell in cities of Greeks and barbarians as the lot of each is cast, and follow the native customs in dress and food and other arrangements of life, yet the constitution of their own citizenship is marvellous and confessedly contradicts expectation. They dwell in their own countries, but only as sojourners; they bear their share in all things as citizens, and they endure all hardships as strangers. Every foreign country is a fatherland to them, and every fatherland is foreign.'

Secular Idealism and the People of God

To many Christians, especially to young adults, this is an attractive picture of what the pattern of Christian relationships should be. Many of them find the argument sometimes put to them by their elders that the Church has a claim on their attention because it is part of their culture, history and national heritage unattractive, even repellent. They think that in these days of change and stress Christians should travel light, with a minimum of cultural baggage and historical impedimenta. Many of them are ready to serve and to make sacrifices in order to express in action their solidarity with those in need. The agencies of the churches whose work helps young nations to their feet or relieves human need find themselves with many willing recruits.

Willingness to serve another church in another nation is part of the growing consciousness of the one people of God. But it is also part of the new-style secular idealism and internationalism of our day. The glaring contrasts between the rich nations which grow richer every day, and the poor growing poorer, are the source of an uneasy conscience among many citizens of countries belonging to the wealthier one-fifth of the world's population. Governments, inter-governmental agencies, wealthy foundations, private philanthropic bodies, are all in the business of supplying either capital or persons to meet the needs of poorer (and usually younger) nations. The mixture of motives scarcely needs description. There is the simple desire to help fellow human-beings; there is the political manoeuvring of great powers; there is the itch for change and adventure; there is the planner's interest in taking a large situation and moulding and shaping it to ends of productivity of one kind or another; there is the trading company's interest; and many more.

One of the most marked contrasts between the India I lived in twenty to thirty years ago and the India I revisited in 1961 was the omnipresence (or so it seemed) on my return of a phenomenon unknown in my time of living in India—the team of experts. At every airport and railway station little groups of brisk Europeans or Americans were being met by deputations armed with garlands. The non-chalance with which the visitors received their cumber-some honours marked them as old hands. It was fun to follow them and pick up the jargon—medical? veterinary? agricultural? forestry? roads? drains? synthetic fibres? It could be anything. Their advice is helping the Indian government to lift some of the load of poverty under which the country staggers.

During my visit I returned to stay at the place where I used to live. I got off the same old train at the same cheerful hour (3 a.m.) into (apparently) the same *jutka* pulled by the same pony, and set out along what I had known as a long and extremely ill-kept road running for several miles under arches of banyan trees with glimpses of moonlit villages and of stars mirrored in the water of the rice fields. Peering out I saw in the glare of an avenue of neon lights large villas, declaring the advent of a new middle class, and nearer to the town, offices and factories covering the ground in unrecognizable profusion.

It took time to find the old tumble-down house in which we had lived: it was overshadowed by gigantic water tanks announcing the arrival of what had been so urgently needed for years—a piped water supply. Everywhere was industrialization and change. An old town that had been very much of a character with its hand industries and its mango groves looked like half the other cities I have seen in various parts of the world. For the middle classes, for those among the poor who have brains and luck, there is opening opportunity. But here, and in the villages, the poor shuffled along the edges of the same odoriferous drains (concreted, maybe, but still open) and many children were barefoot and sore-eyed, and the tenuous grasp of life, which is all that the very poor anywhere have, seemed not to have tightened by so much as a finger's hold. It is mainly from among people such as these that God has called his people into existence in India.

This experience of India revisited puts in the form of a personal experience—shared by many other people—the question raised in an earlier chapter. The people of God is spread abroad over the world; but inter-penetrating the world's life, what influence does it bear? Is it engaging or can it engage with the forces that are shaping a universal civilization based on science and technology, in which planning of both natural and human resources plays so large a part? Is it true, as Dr Visser 't Hooft said recently, that 'the gulf between Christian thinking and the forces shaping our civilization seems to be growing wider all the time'? If this is true (and it is difficult to argue convincingly that it is not broadly true, though with certain exceptions), then how does the Church make its contacts, and what does it stand for in the engagement, and what does it stand against?

Of course, a ready answer to Dr 't Hooft's contention would be to counter him with the question: 'Why should the Church want to shape civilization, or even influence the forces that are shaping it? Is it not the Church's business to go on with its worship and work, no matter what happens?' If 'the Church' means the functions reserved to the clergy, this might be a legitimate answer. But the real issue is that Christians are among the planners, organizers,

directors, teachers, scientists and technologists who are
shaping this new 'world'. Is the fact that they are Christians irrelevant to what they do in all these capacities? If
not—if, that is to say, their calling as Christians is to see
themselves as God's people in this world—then it matters
very much how they view this world of a universal civilization and act in it.

God the Creator of this our World

It is tempting at that point to plunge into a large number
of details about the duties of the laity in their many and
various worldly professions. But if our actions are going to
be theologically grounded our thinking has to begin theologically. What, in theological terms, can be said of this
'world'? It makes an enormous *practical* difference whether
the Christian regards the world as a place where God is
already at work and what kind of action he believes God
to be taking. When he goes out to work all day in a secular
institution with non-Christian companions does he, so to
speak, take God with him or find him already there?

The starting point of a theology of the relation of the
people of God to the world which they inter-penetrate, is
the faith that this world, here and now, is God's world.
The doctrine of creation ought to mean far more to a
Christian than that God in the beginning made the universe with its light and darkness and motion, and the
habitable earth and its inhabitants. This restricts God's
action as Creator to that of a first cause—a role completed.

The way in which most of us have been taught the
Bible makes us think of it as *a history*. Asked 'What is the
first book in the Bible?' it would hardly occur to us to
say: 'Do you mean the oldest, the first to be written?' We
would say 'Genesis', not only because it starts on page 1,
but because its opening words are: 'In the beginning . . .'

Similarly the last book of the Bible is that, in our minds, not only because its end is the final page of print, but because through the vision of St John it describes the end of all things, the new heaven and the new earth. Its closing words are the cry of the Church for the coming of that end: 'Amen, Come Lord Jesus'. Between that beginning in Genesis and that end in Revelation we picture like beads on a thread the fall of man from his created status, the call of Abraham to be the father of a chosen people, the long history of the forming of that people, the coming of the Son of God at a particular time and place as the redeemer of man's lost condition, the birth of the Church. This story, with its beginning and end outside history, was for European civilization down the centuries *the* story of the origin of the world and the history of mankind. Darwin's *Origin of Species* was never intended by its author to be a 'secular creation story': but its publication more than any other event signalized the end of the monopoly of Genesis I as 'the explanation of the beginning of things'.

Today that particular problem, at any rate in that form, does not worry Christians perhaps as much as another. The string of beads I have referred to cannot possibly be thought of as the history of mankind. The point is well put by Simone Weil thus: 'In my eyes Christianity is catholic by right but not in fact. So many things are outside it, so many things that I love and do not want to give up, so many things that God loves, otherwise they would not be in existence. All the immense stretches of past centuries, except the last twenty, are among them; all the countries inhabited by coloured races; all secular life in white peoples' countries . . .'[1]

For many people the story of creation and redemption as understood leaves such vast and various achievements

[1] Simone Weil, *Waiting on God* (Routledge & Kegan Paul), p. 26.

of mankind apparently completely outside. Great cultures flourished centuries before Christ, embracing many millions of souls, yet remote from the whole of the Mediterranean world, let alone the particular history of the Hebrews. They raise not only the question: 'Why did God choose the Jews?' but also: 'Granted that God did choose to work in this way, what place in his purpose has all the rest of the world and its history?' It simply will not fit on to the string of beads; there is no way of breaking and rejoining the thread. This compels us to ask ourselves whether we have rightly understood the relationship of creation and redemption if we think of them as being only in a historical sequence.

The idea of an actual creation by God of the universe, the world and its vegetation, animals and inhabitants in the remote past and as a beginning of everything came into Hebrew religion at a late date. The Hebrew prophets wrestled with the problem of a people continually lapsing into the nature-worship of their neighbours and the co-inhabitants of the land. Their message was the recall of the people to the God who had 'brought them up out of the land of Egypt' and made his covenant with them in the desert. He was a God of events, of personal dealings with his people, a God demanding moral performance, a God who leads Israel as a father teaches a tiny child to walk and gathers him up in his arms (Hosea 11.3). 'How can I give you up, O Ephraim! How can I hand you over, O Israel!' This God, says Amos (5.8), is

'He who made the Pleiades and Orion,
and turns deep darkness into the morning
and darkens the day into night,
who calls for the waters of the sea
and pours them out upon the surface of the earth.'

This God, who is known as God acting in history, the loving father as well as the judge, comes to be seen as the Creator of the whole earth. But in the passage quoted the tenses of the verbs are important. God is Creator not only in having made the stars: *every* dawn and nightfall, *every* shower of rain, is a creation. The child who says 'God made me' is talking about the God Hosea knew and not about a first cause working its way down an infinity of generations to this child. We, and all that surrounds us, are made by a divine Father; that the Creator is this kind of a God makes us the persons we are. Delivered from the long pre-occupation with creation as *'how* the world began' we can see again, perhaps more clearly, the universal, perpetual creativity of the Creator who is love, who puts upon everything the mark of love—uniqueness, personality, freedom.

The Creativity of Christ

Thus far we are on common ground with the Jew. But the Christian has his own creation story. Genesis is not the only book in the Bible whose opening words are 'In the beginning'. By deliberate intent St John opens his gospel with the words 'In the beginning'. The word of God, which 'dwelt among us, full of grace and truth' in Jesus Christ was in the beginning 'and through him all things came to be . . . all that came to be was alive with his life, and that life was the light of men.' The life-restoring power of the redeemer of the world is also the life- and light-giving power of creation: and this light which shone in the darkness 'in the beginning' is the same that gives the light of being alive to every man in the world.

Nor is St John alone in re-shaping the doctrine of creation in the light of Christian revelation. St Paul, in the first chapter of the Epistle to the Colossians, does the

same. Everything and every power, temporal or super-
natural, has been made through and for Christ. 'All things
were created through him and for him. He is before all
things and in him all things hold together.' As Professor
Sittler said in his remarkable address to the Third Assembly of the World Council of Churches, this four-times
repeated 'all things' is rapped out in the Greek in a way
which leaves us in no doubt of the meaning—nothing falls
outside the range of his action.

It is for this reason that some theologians begin to talk
more nowadays of 'the cosmic Christ', that is to say, of
the work of Christ in relation to the whole world of nature
and history. This is no sort of Christian pantheism, seeing
Christ present in everything as a pervasive force divorced
from the actual historical events of his incarnation. It
arises not only from the passages I have quoted which link
the divine word, the redeemer, with the creative power of
God, but also from a number of passages in the New
Testament in which the historical events of the incarnation,
and especially the cross and resurrection, are seen also as
cosmic events with cosmic effects. St Paul says in the
Epistle to the Romans that the whole universe 'groans in
all its parts as if in the pangs of childbirth', and he adds
that 'even we, to whom the Spirit is given . . ., are groaning
while we wait for God to make us his sons and set our
whole body free'. The physical body is part of the physical
world created by God. Hebrew thought never tolerated or
even entertained the idea that man was a spirit in a body
and that God had to do with 'the spirit'. To Hebrew thinking man is 'a living soul', a totality of inseparable parts. In
modern scientific jargon, he is a psychosomatic whole.
Redemption therefore, says St Paul, is not of man out of
his body and out of the physical world which sustains his
bodily life. 'All things', his own body and his physical

environment, are included in the redeeming work of Christ.

The author of the Epistle to the Hebrews saw the action of God in Christ as retroactive in time. The men of old time so wonderfully described in Hebrews 11 did not receive the promise which was fulfilled in Christ. But because they were men of faith they do receive it along with those who, having had the Gospel preached to them, trust in Christ.

Yet another aspect of the total cosmic drama of salvation appears in the vision of St John. There is 'war in heaven' and 'that old serpent', the deceiver of men and their accuser before God (as in the book of Job), is thrown out of heaven, defeated (Rev. 12.7). This defeated enemy lashes out in fury against the followers of his enemy the Lamb: but although he works terrible havoc in the Church and in the world, playing all the time the role of the deceiver who draws men's worship away from God to the worship of men and of men's power and authority, yet he cannot change the issue of that heavenly struggle. His days are numbered; in the words of the dying Saviour on the cross, IT IS ACCOMPLISHED.

The people of God in the world are not therefore those who despair of their earthly life, or of the earth their bodily home, or of mankind whose sins are already taken away by the Lamb of God, the Son of God and Saviour of the world (John 1.29; I John 2.2). But, of course, for Christians in the world the New Testament is full of warnings of tribulation. There will be misrepresentation, obloquy, blame for every disaster, accusations of disloyalty to the state, of falsehood, of sinister practices, and these lead on to fanatical hatred, persecution, martyrdom. These are to be expected, says Jesus, and the absence of them is reason for self-examination. The New Testament speaks of 'the world' in one sense as 'under the power of the evil one', and there are many references to the prince of this world or the powers of this world militating against the power of the spirit.

This New Testament conception of a present age when, as St John in his vision saw, a defeated enemy is lashing out, sits very uneasily with notions of history which we consider 'normal'. It is vital that we should understand the meaning of the New Testament distinction between the world of men for which Christ died and the age (often translated 'world') when the powers of evil hurl themselves against God, a time in which the final victory of Christ is assured but not accomplished. Failure to understand this distinction contributes a good deal to a kind of dualism to be found among some Christians today. The struggle between good and evil in the world seems to them to be a gigantic struggle whose outcome is uncertain. Such dualism has no warrant in scripture or Christian doctrine: nor has its opposite, the notion that evil is in some sense 'unreal'. William James once silenced an argument with the comment: 'However you may explain it, it feels like a real struggle.' It is 'a real struggle' for every Christian committed by his baptismal vows 'to continue Christ's faithful soldier and servant unto his life's end'. Many engagements and battles are lost in a war whose final outcome is sure, and the final victory is delayed by these losses.

As the people of God we set out therefore daily in the confidence that every situation is given to us by God; that the people of God are in relation to the world not 'the goodies' versus 'the baddies', but the people to whom, in the incredible mercy of God, is entrusted a *secret,* that is the knowledge of God's act of love towards the whole world which he made in Christ and makes all the time. One of the temptations to which Christians are subject is

that of interpreting the secret as a private agreement between Christians and God, as though God's offer to the
world was that he would keep a place for a Christian warm
and secure amid the storms of life. What God offers is, on
the contrary, a share in the sufferings of Christ in and for
the world.

This often evokes the wrong picture of a Christ suffering
because he was beaten and defeated, deprived by men of
any alternative possibilities, calling on his followers to
renounce the creative possibilities of life in the world and
become as helpless as he was. This is a travesty of the
meaning of Passion, for Christ's passion was on the God-
ward side the most tremendous action. In it the one who
could most powerfully have resisted the will of God because he was the Son, put himself wholly and voluntarily
at the disposal of God's will. We cannot possibly understand what it means that the all-holy God should come
among men who were bound, in their unholiness, to reject
him. The descent described in Philippians 2 is like the
swoop of an eagle: though in the form of God, Christ does
not grasp the equality with God which is his by right, but
empties himself into the form of a servant and is born a
man and then on downwards to share a man's death, and
not only death, but the utter degradation of death on a
cross, outside the city, outside his own people. Only from
within mankind, beside and with men, can God breach the
wall that man has erected between himself and God, that
is to say, between himself and the source of his life, and
between himself and his fellow men. 'My father worketh
hitherto', says Jesus, 'and I work.' So Christ asks us to
share his sufferings in a world in which he is continuously
at work. The promise to be with us comes from one who is
always in front of us and beckons us on.

Our Calling and Our Work

What is God calling us to be in his world? In the course of my work I often receive letters from people who want to change their jobs. Such a possibility is only open to a very small minority of people. For the great majority there is no choice, or there is an initial choice which, once made, sets the pattern of the work pursued all through life. The possibility of a wide range of choice in work is opened by the possession of money and influence or (increasingly) of intelligence and education. The Church exists as an institution possessed of a certain number of full-time posts: it needs persons of competence and devotion to fill them. Unfortunately, a good deal of confusion is caused by this fact, and many people think that God's call means a call to a particular job, and especially to a job in church employment or, as many put it, to 'a job with people' (teaching, nursing, social work). God's call to us through Christ is simply to trust him, to worship him, to commit our lives to him. The change in our condition effected by our calling is not that we give up doing whatever we are doing and do something else, but that we are 'delivered from the dominion of darkness and transferred to the kingdom of his beloved Son'.

There is a great hankering in many of us for some special call of God to some special work for him. The New Testament speaks often of our high calling in Christ Jesus. There are many parables of men called to the kingdom of God. The secular use of the words 'calling' and 'vocation' to mean the work a man does never suggests that there is a divine caller. But we distort the meaning of Christian vocation if we merely take the secular idea of a calling and add God's name to it. Secular 'calling' has as its most distinctive feature the separation of one person from another into one training, profession and job or another. One of the most important aspects of the people of God is our *solidarity* of calling to be his sons. God asks of the man of very great ability and standing in the world's affairs exactly what he asks of the poorest Indian outcaste —his life, to be at God's disposal. God cannot ask more of any man, nor can any man give more.

For members of mainly middle class churches this solidarity is not easy to see. A Presbyterian minister comments: 'The word "laity" is not customarily used in churches of our order. Its coming into our vocabulary is forcing us to think of things we do not very much want to think about—our solidarity and collectivity, for example, over against the individuality of our usual ways of thinking of "church members".' Whatever our church order, it is very difficult for Westerners, with their deeply ingrained individualism and their temptation to think of themselves as the bearers of civilization and the solvers of the world's problems, to admit this common calling. What more can we do than put ourselves, our gifts and circumstances, at God's disposition? What we often refer to as our Christian 'calling' to be a doctor or teacher or lawyer could be better understood as God's use of gifts he has given us and our willingness to put them at his disposal.

Our common calling brings into one fellowship in the Church rich and poor, the planner and the planned, the teacher and the taught. We shall have to turn in the next chapter to the question whether in fact we are within listening distance of one another in the fellowship of the Church, but here we must look at some of the features that have developed as individual Christians and churches have begun to take seriously the calling of the Church to be the people of God in the world, in the place where they are.

There are two different kinds of group in existence concerned with Christians in their work. One type draws together Christians within a profession, to pray together and study the Bible, usually in their place of work or near it; the other is the group which aims at working out for the guidance of its own members what it means to be a Christian within a given profession—what the important decisions are and what the Christian should be standing for or opposing. The first kind of group is often very important, especially to young Christians flung into an entirely new kind of life when they leave school and go to work. Every type of church has developed such groups, from the Roman Catholic Young Catholic Workers to the Evangelical Unions. Their problem is how to avoid being the holy huddle cut off, by the absorption of time, from their non-Christian fellows. Any group of one profession and almost entirely of one age and status lacks the richness and the mutual correction of a group meeting within the church. The other type of group turns its attention towards the world, and tackles the questions of the Christian engagement in the sphere of professional activity. It is not usually local.

This second type of group has often penetrated really deeply into problems of responsibility, decision-making, and day-to-day conduct. But such groups need theological assistance, especially in handling the Bible in the very difficult matter of applying its teaching without distorting it. There are, however, real limits to what a professional group can do. One such limit arises from the complexity of modern structures. Few professional people work entirely independently: a large and growing number are employed in industry, or in departments of local or central government, or in the armed services, or in education. In each case they are part of a large organism made up of people of widely different professional and non-professional backgrounds and competence. The cost accountant, the company solicitor, the sales manager and the works manager may have rather sharply divided views on general policy and on particular applications.

A search for criteria in organizations is always going on. In some cases it is comparatively simple. One demands of a fire service efficiency in putting out fires, and this takes priority over everything else. One would be unlikely to find a defender for the view that old ladies might excusably be allowed to burn in their beds if the firemen were too busy at their Bible study to hear the alarm! But in more complicated structures criteria are far less easily reduced to such simplicity.

A large factory exists to produce goods for customers of the best quality and (so the customer wishes) at the lowest price. But it is not only a building full of machines, but an interlocking series of departments, each with its horizontal affiliations to other departments along the levels of status: and all is within the total structure of the firm, embracing everyone from the Chairman of the Board of Directors to the nightwatchman, and everything from the electronic computor to the cups in the canteen. In addition to its responsibilities to the broad categories of shareholders, customers and employees, it also has obligations to the country and to the local community. Its laboratories and research staff may be making a substantial contribution to scientific knowledge, and its philanthropies contribute to education, welfare, the arts and the Church. Furthermore, it is the educator of a group of apprentices and other young people, and the welfare service of the sick, the injured and the aging. There is not a single criterion of operation which, pressed too far, will not exact too high a price in the sacrifice of other criteria.

Consumers who want electric lamps are not going to be lenient to the plea that the lamps are bad but the personal relations are good. People are not going to give of their best if they sense that efficiency or output is put consistently before human values—indeed, they may withhold their work altogether. But often the sense of being treated as a person depends on such highly technical things as organizing the flow of work in such a way that people are not alternately left standing idle and rushed off their feet. It may depend on small things—proper lights, clean lavatories, adequate first aid. It may be completely frustrated by the inability of management to overcome the blocks in communication which are a major problem in large organizations.

It is important to attempt to clarify Christian objectives, although these will constantly change in outward form. Two centuries ago an entirely fatalistic determinism dominated emerging industrial life. People were sacrificed to machines not only because of personal greed, but out of a conviction that only prodigious hours of labour at fabulously low wages would keep the goods flowing and return the capital laid out. Compared to that, an atmosphere of astonishing freedom prevails today. We have far greater assurance that industry can be made to serve the need of the community for goods, and of the working group for a good wage and good conditions.

The work of a manager in industry, of a trade union official or any person holding responsibility for the ordering of relationships may do much to remove the occasions of bitterness, strife, anger and panic. If this were being done by Christians we should regard it as a work of Christ: but we ought to be able to say that we recognize it as Christ's work no matter what the personal beliefs of the agents. The Christian should surely see it as part of the function of making straight paths for our feet and removing stones of stumbling. Very small actions not only of kindness but of competence, promptitude and restraint by innumerable people make it possible to live and work together. If we truly believed that Christ is at work in such actions we would neither want credit for ourselves nor grudge it to others.

> 'Christ is *incognito* already present in the structures and power systems in which we have to live our Christian life. Not all powers and principalities are against God. When we speak about Christ to our neighbours and colleagues who are not church members, it is never a one-way communication. Christ is between us and teaches us both. When in our daily work we fulfil our task in the welfare state together with our non-Christian colleagues, Christ serves not only through us but also through them.' [1]

It is idle for the Christian to pretend to any superior knowledge coming from his faith, showing the rightness or wrongness of this industrial policy or that. Like everyone else, the Christian has to work to know and understand a total situation and his place in it. His objective can probably best be described as securing the greatest amount of justice for the largest number of people, and especially for those who have been deprived of it. He works for this justice as a member of an organized group. His consciousness of his calling out of darkness into the kingdom of God's Son does not make him an outsider to any situation: it makes him doubly an insider, because he sees that a struggle of tremendous importance is going on. His own job of work will claim his full attention: he is working

[1] Statement on *The Laity: the Church in the World* made by three lay people to the Third Assembly of the World Council of Churches, 1961.

with a people and materials who are, like him, struggling towards a new birth.

As the Christian works he will be confronted by the paradox that just when the freedom to make industry serve genuinely human ends is greater than before, large numbers of people have lost all sense of meaning in work. It is done for a wage, and endured. Even young people leaving school do not look forward to finding any satisfaction in work. No doubt this is partly due to circumstances—to the futility of so many of the goods produced, to the lack of any share in the end-product of one's work; but it seems to be more than that—an accidie or lethargy such as afflicted the old monks. In this situation the Christian's attitude to his own work may be important. It should not be for him either a mere way of earning a living in order to be somewhere else doing something else, or a device for meeting other people and evangelizing them. His work must become the subject of his prayers. It takes much grace to accept modern work gladly as from God. But if we think that work in some time past gave every man satisfactions hidden from us today, we ought to think again. If work was really all that 'meaningful' or 'satisfying' or all the other words that are used, why were men such fools as to go to the inordinate trouble and expense of getting slaves to do it for them?

None of the characteristic Christian approaches to work can be made easily relevant at any time. To Luther, engagement in economic activity is the first, most important way in which a Christian serves his neighbour. We can hardly imagine the 'neighbour' at the end of most of our long-drawn lines of economic activity; but it was just as hard to serve the neighbour you knew and disliked! We surely have to learn to serve our neighbour by our work as well as by our voluntary efforts through giving time and money. To Calvinist thinking, work was obedience to God's commands. A quality of 'dourness' in certain present attitudes to work marks the continuation of this influence, but at its best it contained an emphasis on personal responsibility to God for one's work which was the best element in the 'rugged individualism' we now seem less happy to commend. The Catholic and main Anglican attitude makes work an offering of worship. It belongs with a sacramental view of life, in which everything is a gift for the altar: but it has never been easy to see what constitutes a worthy offering.

There is nothing we so much need as a doctrine of work which not only helps Christians, but makes some contribution to the present situation. It is hard to believe that a man can write off as meaningless the activity to which he devotes his best waking hours and which gives him not only his livelihood but his standing in society and sense of worth in it, without suffering a deep deprivation in his whole being. Yet this is undoubtedly where we are. The gulf is widening between the type of work which exacts everything from a man that he has to give and absorbs him wholly, and the type of work which asks little or nothing and gives little or nothing. The only place where this problem can be tackled is in industry and education, and especially in the relations between the two. Our danger is that we regard persons capable of the first type of work (in all its many degrees and aspects) as the main objects of our educational system, and the rest as those who failed to come up to the required standard.

A chief characteristic of an industrial society is to release enormous surpluses of goods, time and energy *after* the satisfaction of basic human needs. Our frustrations arise very largely from the inordinate expectations we possess and from our disappointment that machines increase our desires as much as they decrease our labours. To curb our inordinate desires, even the desire for doing inordinate good, is part of a Christian discipline of today. For Christians may fall into the temptation of sharing the exaggerated moral aspirations of a secular society which has replaced humble faith by arrogant belief in its own large possibilities of doing good. Not content with being men, men since the Enlightenment at the end of the eighteenth century have wanted to be supermen, better than men really are, and miraculously delivered from the self-defeating elements in all human efforts after goodness. This is the source of one of the major issues dividing the political East from the political West. The West is largely dominated by this post-Enlightenment moral idealism. It prevails as widely in the United States, where church-going is the habit of the majority, as in Britain where it is not. There is no limit to what the good man can do if he wishes (so the argument runs), and would do if he were not perpetually inhibited by the hangover of Christian warnings, denigrations, and crippling self-distrust. Nietzsche was the main exponent of these ideas and he has many followers even today.

The East sees in the West a situation reduceable to the simple formula 'exaggerated statement + indifferent achievement = hypocrisy' and pursues its own conclusion: power, not idealism, is the true reality; therefore embrace it without the hypocrisy of excuses, confident that the forces of history operating through the steady pressure of the mass of the dispossessed will put power into the hands of those ready to take and use it.

The question 'What is man?' enters into the heart of every contemporary debate. The question can be answered theologically, but the answer can only commend itself to

men as they see it lived. It cannot be lived except in the
world and by the people of God.

To many Christian lay people Dietrich Bonhoeffer's
Letters and Papers from Prison has become a well-worn
and trusty friend. In its pages—never intended for publication—one sees a theologian and pastor, a 'churchman'
if ever there was one, responding with all the concentration of a trained mind and a sensitive spirit to the situation of being thrust into prison in the company of men of
many different types. After more than two years of imprisonment without trial, he was executed on April 9th,
1945. One of the last to see him was an English fellow-
prisoner, who said of him: 'He always seemed to me to
diffuse an atmosphere of happiness, of joy in every small-
est event of life, of deep gratitude for the mere fact that he
was alive ... He was one of the very few men I have ever
met to whom his God was real and close to him.'

In spite of the brevity of his writing, Bonhoeffer has become the theologian who speaks most clearly to the condition of those who are exploring the meaning of the presence and ministry of the people of God in the secular
world. One of his last letters contains these words:

'During the last year or so I have come to appreciate
the "worldliness" of Christianity as never before. The
Christian is not a *homo religiosus*, but a man, pure
and simple, just as Jesus was a man, compared with
John the Baptist anyhow. I don't mean the shallow
this-worldliness of the enlightened, of the busy, the
comfortable or the lascivious. It's something much
more profound than that, something in which the
knowledge of death and resurrection is ever present ...
I remember talking to a young French pastor at A.
thirteen years ago. We were discussing what our real
purpose was in life. He said he would like to become a
saint. I think it is quite likely he did become one. At the

time I was very much impressed, though I disagreed with him and said I should prefer to have faith, or words to that effect. For a long time I did not realize how far we were apart. I thought I could acquire faith by trying to live a holy life, or something like it . . .

'Later I discovered and am still discovering up to this very moment that it is only by living completely in this world that one learns to believe. One must abandon every attempt to make something of oneself, whether it be a saint, a converted sinner, a churchman (the priestly type, so-called!), a righteous man or an unrighteous one, a sick man or a healthy one. This is what I mean by worldliness—taking life in one's stride, with all its duties and problems, its successes and failures, its experiences and helplessness. It is in such a life that we throw ourselves utterly into the arms of God and participate in his sufferings in the world and watch with Christ in Gethsemane. That is faith, that is *metanoia*, and that is what makes a man and a Christian (cf. Jeremiah 45). How can success make us arrogant or failure lead us astray, when we participate in the sufferings of God by living in this world?' [1]

---

[1] *Letters and Papers from Prison*, pp. 168-9. (Fontana ed., pp. 124-5).

8

THE CONGREGATION AND THE
PEOPLE OF GOD

Clerical and Lay Ministries in the World

ONLY the whole Church, not the laity by itself, can claim to be 'the people of God'. If we accept this statement and the full logic of it, we cannot accept some of the contemporary definitions of the difference in the place of its exercise between the 'ministry of the clergy' and the 'ministry of the laity'. According to these the laity have their ministry out in the world. The clergy are ministers in the parish or congregation. The congregation is the 'base camp' where the clergy prepare the laity for their ministry in the world by arming and sustaining them with word and sacraments, teaching and pastoral care. This looks like a very neat theory. But it would not look so neat if we remembered our Greek priest hoeing his field, or the men being ordained in India who earn their living as farmers or shopkeepers. In other words, we often make statements about the difference between clergy and laity which have nothing to do with ordination but are really distinctions between 'full-timers' and 'part-timers' in the service of the Church.

It is really urgent that we now assert fully that *both the ordained and the lay ministry are ministries in and to the world,* within the wholeness of the people of God. Many lay people are nowadays quite rightly complaining about the ingrown character of some church life. 'I am appalled', writes one of them, 'at some of the activities gathered round the local church. They seem to belong much more to the drawing room of a Victorian vicarage than to the modern world.'[1] With rather more violence an American writes: 'The clergyman finds that many of the most sensitive and honest men and women in his parish feel that the patterns of piety and the programmes of the local church are inane, if not positively offensive . . . I think we are beginning to see a kind of lay revolt.'[2]

We shall have to take up the question whether this is a revolt against the parish as such, or against what many parishes or congregations do. But first it is necessary to say that the 'revolt' is not only or chiefly by the laity. Clergy are also in revolt against the double suggestion which seems to be in the air with all the talk of the importance of the laity. First, that the congregation or parish as we know it has no future, and second, that 'the parson's place is in the parish'. Why, then, should men accept ordination in the first place or, if ordained, turn to the parochial ministry as their life work?

There is a growing volume of evidence that many young men think about the ordained ministry and come to the sober conclusion that they will do better service for the Kingdom of God as laymen, at any rate while they are young. A British theological professor spoke recently of ' . . . a noticeable tendency among men preparing for the ministry to put off entry into the parochial ministry for one reason or another: they must, they say, take another degree, or go into industry for a year to get some experience of the world, or become teachers of divinity in schools'. For four months last year 700 theological students in Athens university were on strike: their protest

---

[1] A layman writing in answer to an enquiry undertaken by the Church of England Board of Education in reference to lay training.
[2] Joseph Duffey, Assistant Director of the Institute of Church and Community, at Hartford, Connecticut, USA.

was against changes proposed by the government in the religious teaching in state schools which would have closed this employment to them. 'Notice how often seminarians are loath to speak of entering the parish ministry...', writes an American seminary teacher. 'Many express doubts that they can "take the pressures of the parish ministry".'

Among those who are in the parochial ministry (using the word 'parochial' to mean a ministry within a congregation or group of congregations, whatever the denomination), an increasing number undertake paid employment outside their parochial work partly, but not only, for economic reasons. They argue that it takes them out where people are and gives them opportunities of converse with non-Christians. About five hundred ordained men in England are working as full-time teachers in state schools.

It seems to me that there are real dangers of lay arrogance in an attitude which seems to say to the clergy: 'We do the real fighting: you prepare us for it.' An attitude which regards the parson as the domestic chaplain to the faithful is quite as erroneous as one which regards the laity as the 'backers-up' of the clergy. Many of the great missionaries and pioneer evangelists have been clergy, so have the founders and heads of schools in this country and abroad. Clergy have had their part in the intellectual debates and encounters with the Church's attackers, they have written some of the best books on the Church and the social order.

It must be admitted that this activity of clergy in relation to the world has declined in recent years. We have fewer clergy, and caring for the parishes and congregations is laid on them as the first claim and duty. But we should be wrong to accept that as inevitable. Far more can, and should, be done to rationalize our situation in regard to numbers of church buildings. We have in fact far more church buildings (i.e. local churches and their accompanying halls, rooms, etc.), in proportion to the population in England than there are in the USA, in spite of the fact that the church-going proportion of the nation is at least three times as large there as here. We need to deal radically with this problem, by working for the unity of the churches and by reorganizing church life even before unity is achieved. Instead of imprisoning the clergy in serving too many pieces of organization, we should release more for the demands of work in colleges, schools, universities, hospitals, prisons, industry and the 'para-parochial' experiments of our day.

The whole people of God has a ministry in and to the world. That means that the parson, like Chaucer's 'parson of the towne', has his role in the world as well as in the gathered congregation. It is part of the duty of lay people to encourage and enable him to fulfil it. It means also that the layman should be concerned, along with the clergy, to think about the future role of the congregation, of Sunday and what happens on Sunday, in the total life of the Church which is the presence of God's people in the world.

For this to happen there has to be a mutuality of regard for the lay and the clerical life within the people of God. *Lay people* must not be led to think that daily work is important only because, or in so far as, it offers opportunities for evangelism. Earning a living, working to produce goods or services, playing one's part in making the working community as far as possible a true community of persons—these are all activities of response to God's creation of the world through Christ. *Clergy* are, in a world which has so largely rejected God, the visible reminders of this rejection. That is one of the reasons why they suffer ridicule and attack. Yet they are constantly meeting men and women at the points in their lives where many of them still want to remember, want to keep open by a narrow chink a door back to active faith. All Christians are called to minister to the world, but clergy are entrusted on behalf of us all with the exceptional means of confirming forgiveness, of holding out to us the means of illumination and grace in scripture and sacraments, and of maintaining the Church in the fullness of the truth of the faith.

Laymen and clergymen should have no positions to maintain over against each other within a people of God rejected by the world and committed to serving it.

Why the Local Congregation?

In such a situation as that of our day, we have to ask 'Why the local congregation at all?' and 'What is the inescapable basic minimum?' We are moving now out of a period in which it was generally considered that a congregation should do as much as possible, filling every moment of Sunday and every week evening with activities, into one of asking: 'What must be done in a gathered congregation and how much is better done elsewhere?'

These phases of church life are capable of study, by social historians, and we owe an immense debt to French Roman Catholic writers who have so clearly shown the pattern of this development in different parts of France. All of it has been directed towards the problem of living as a Christian in a country which felt earlier than any other the full force of the rejection of the Church and the faith by large sections of the population. The France of the *ancien régime* was a country of peasant piety and worldly nobility. In the nineteenth century the bourgeoisie made their mark felt in the Church: many parishes became bourgeois parishes. But the revolutionary attack on the Church left deep scars. Radical scepticism allied itself

with the attack on residual privilege. In the early years of
this century the attack on the Church took on a renewed
sharpness. After bitter abuse of the Church, education became completely secularized. The religious orders were
either expelled or banned from teaching.

One of the first reactions of the Church was to strengthen
certain parishes and to create a range of Catholic
organizations. So in Paris it was possible to live from a
Catholic cradle to a Catholic grave in a Catholic school,
trade union, youth club and political party. The Church
took the young as far as possible out of the world and into
the highly organized Church—but the young had, of
course, still to work in the world and feel its pressures.

The next phase was therefore that of the *Jocists*—the
Young Catholic Workers—with their parallel movements
among farmers, sailors, students and many other groups.
Great rallies and meetings called attention to the number
and solidarity of young Catholics. Priests as chaplains
worked wholly with these young workers and the desire of
closer identification of the priest with the scattered Church
of the Catholics in the vast industries of France led
to the 'worker priests'. The decline of the *Jocists* (which
suffered, like every youth movement, from the marrying,
settling down, and ageing of the pioneer generation) and
the consciousness that the parishes were, after all, *still
there*, weak and unrelated to all this, led to an attempt to
bring a new emphasis into parish life. The book *Revolution in a City Parish* tells the story of the Abbé
Michonneau and the directing of the life of a parish outwards towards the world.

Success in one field, however, did not blind the eyes of
French Catholics to the vast, unyielding structures of
modern life, to the huge factories and office blocks, and
the great housing estates where it was not possible to

gather a Christian congregation, where a priest roused no reaction but blind and ignorant abuse. Here, then, began in 1950 the *Action Catholique Ouvrière* and the 'Secular Institutes' of lay men and women working full-time in secular jobs, wearing ordinary dress, taking adapted vows (so that a doctor's 'poverty' would include a car), making their retreats as they could, and directed by directors of a different stamp. They see themselves as communicators; their first task is to bring to secular life a spiritual vitality and awakening and so to make 'a Christian' mean someone who so shares every one of the pressures of life on ordinary people that he can be talked to. *Opus Dei*, with its roots in Spain, belongs also in this part of the picture of Catholic Action.

Sociological study carried out by Catholics, including priests truly competent to do the scientific work, has been of tremendous assistance to all this endeavour. The heart of it is the conviction, confirmed by study, that France is 'a mission country'. We cannot jump to the conclusion that England, with its different history, is precisely the same: but to a very large extent we operate in the dark, and a book like Bishop Wickham's *Church and People in an Industrial City*, with its scholarly treatment of history, comes on us as a welcome and too rare illumination. It is sad that a country which produced the greatest of all sociological surveys of the place of religion in a vast city[1] should have fallen so far behind.

Nevertheless, if we cannot know our situation so confidently as the French, we can take the broad outline of their conclusion, which is that *we cannot let the parish church or gathered congregation go, and we cannot rely on it to do everything that can be or needs to be done.*

[1] *London Life and Labour* by Charles Booth, a pioneer layman, published in the 1890s.

It is legitimate and necessary to go back to the roots and to ask 'why the local congregation, and for what'?

The Laity and Worship

Bishop Lilje of Hanover, himself a strong protagonist of many efforts designed to help the laity fulfil their ministry in the world, put the matter in a nutshell. 'If Christians come together for worship, and clearly this is their first duty, then they must come together in some one place. The very fact of worship constitutes a local congregation. Can there be a church which is not local?' Only by going Sunday by Sunday together do we begin to put into a corporate act of worship what it really asks of us if it is to be a worthy offering to God.

This is one of the reasons why those who only go to church at infrequent intervals complain that they 'can't understand what's going on'. They have a legitimate grouse against archaic language left unexplained, and not every congregation helps the occasional comer to become a participating worshipper. But basically the point is sound that without the will to make an offering of worship jointly with others, one remains on the fringes of the Church's worship. It is those who have learned to bring this attitude to worship who are able to make the transition from one congregation to another that modern life makes unavoidable. If worship is to be the central activity of the Church, then the laity must moderate their claims on the clergy for pastoral care, 'activities' and 'saying a few words at . . .' in such a way that they can give to public worship all that it demands of private preparation.

A local church is also a baptismal community: indeed a local church exists as much for baptism as for the eucharist. Baptism is *the* symbol of dying with Christ a death to sin and rising with him to new life. A baptism, even if it takes place at home or in a hospital ward, is baptism into the Church and the community of the Church is responsible for that nurture and instruction which from the earliest times has been the accompaniment of baptism. Vows are taken by or on behalf of the baptized and in the face of witnesses who are present as or on behalf of the Church. Infant baptism carries with it an obligation on the local church to nurture that child in the faith: this it delegates to parents and godparents who are to act for the Church. *As the baptismal community, the congregation must be a congregation of families.* This is the strongest argument for saying that a local congregation must be local to where people live, that is to where they have their families.

Adult baptism equally demands an active role by the local congregation in nurture and instruction. The pentecostal sects have a lesson for us all in this matter, for they have brought baptism into the centre of the life of the congregation, making both the witness of the baptized, and their instruction, a central part of worship. The degradation of baptism into a naming ceremony and a social custom robs us of what a sacrament ought to give us—an apprehension of a spiritual truth without words of explanation. Passing through the Red Sea made the escaping children of Israel a people. The waters closed upon their enemy as they walked out of them on to the land.[1] Baptism is incorporation into the people of God. Christ, who submitted himself to baptism by John, spoke of the baptism of his passion and death. To belong to the Body of Christ through baptism means therefore incorporation into Christ *in his suffering for men*. We are baptized into

[1] F. W. Dillistone, in *Christianity and Symbolism*, suggests that the baptism of proselytes by Jews before the time of Christ was a dramatic re-enactment of passing through the Red Sea, so that they might become part of the people of God.

his *flock* which he gathers into his fold, and into his *army* which is committed to battle in the world.[1]

The Laity and Teaching

Worship, and especially eucharistic worship and baptism, with nurture and teaching which should accompany it—these make a regularly gathering congregation the indispensable 'base' of the life of the people of God in the world. Most would say that equally important is 'the ministry of the word' for which the ordained ministry is set aside equally with the ministry of the sacraments. Commonly this 'ministry of the word' is almost entirely identified with preaching. 'Take thou authority', says the Anglican bishop at the ordination of a priest, 'to *preach* the word of God'. This is no place to enter into the varieties of kinds of preaching and the role of preaching in worship. The point here is that the sermon is usually the main part of the teaching done in most congregations. In a recent small survey of lay opinion [2] none of the topics touched upon evoked such unanimity of response—unanimity not of criticism but of puzzlement. What is preaching for? How can the sermon possibly be used as the main teaching medium in congregations composed, as most are, of widely different ages, ranges of experience or knowledge and spiritual needs? The warmth of appreciation of (and the length of memory for) a particular sermon show why the laity ask for a ministry of the word. But there was also an insistence that the ministry of the

[1] 'We receive this Child into the congregation of Christ's flock, and do sign him with the sign of the Cross, in token that hereafter he shall not be ashamed to confess the faith of Christ crucified, and manfully to fight under his banner, against sin, the world, and the devil; and to continue Christ's faithful soldier and servant unto his life's end.' *Book of Common Prayer*.

[2] By the Church of England Board of Education.

word cannot in modern conditions be fulfilled only by preaching.

The gap between clergy and laity in general education has closed significantly everywhere: in some congregations completely so. But in other respects it has widened dangerously because a knowledge of the contents of the Bible by the laity cannot be taken for granted any more. When the Bible was first read aloud in English in churches, people crowded to the front to hear what they had never heard before. Progressively after the Reformation the Bible became the layman's handbook which he could read in the light of his general education. Indeed the Bible was itself a substantial part of his education. The shift of the content of education in our own day towards acquiring knowledge and skills for living in a technical society make it less of a help than it was when it contained far more history, drama and poetry and when these were regarded as a key to understanding man. The laity therefore need help to re-grasp and use the great truths of the Bible. New translations have made the meaning of the words clearer, but the strangeness of the ideas often seems even more startling. We cannot simply abandon the effort to come to terms with the Bible. Our worship is so rooted and grounded in it that if we cannot understand the Bible we cannot understand what we are doing in worship either. Nor have we any other source of knowledge of the revelation of God in Christ.

The question of the ministry of the word leads therefore into the question of the whole teaching ministry of the Church.

Before he wrote *The Organization Man*, William Whyte wrote another work called *Is Anybody Listening?* It is partly about advertising, but mostly about the problem of communicating ideas and information within an organization. His thesis, based upon the study of a number of American organizations, is that success in being heard depends to a very large degree on the practice of listening. A management which does not listen and make deliberate provision for doing so cannot get itself heard because it is unversed in the language in which alone it could be understood and fails to understand the basic fact that people take things in as a part of a dialogue to which they are quite impervious if they are presented as a statement. This thesis has stood the test of further examination. It is important for the Church (and, indeed, Whyte included some congregations in his enquiry).

If a teaching Church can only become that by being a listening Church, what provision are we making for listening? This does not mean 'the clergy must listen to the laity'; it means that the Church gathered for worship and teaching, including the laity in their churchly frame of mind, must listen to the people of God in the world, themselves scattered abroad, and also to the non-Christian neighbour in the world. Teaching in the Church ought to take the form in which the laity have to stand up for their faith in the world, that is in dialogue. The laity are aware that their explanations often fail to convince, that they are countered by questions they cannot answer, that situations arise in the world to which faith seems irrelevant, that much of the personal morality taught in the Church cannot be translated straight into the situations of group responsibility, decision and action which predominate in considerable areas of life. They have to grapple with problems of family breakdown, young people going adrift, illness, death, crisis, and boredom. All this must be said within the teaching life of the congregation. It is not enough to say 'let us have group discussion'. People can make speeches in groups just as well as from platforms and the groups in which people really listen at depth are not common.

But we can increase their number. We are beginning in the churches to take advantage of new knowledge of how to communicate with one another within groups, not in order to become propagandists armed with techniques of brainwashing, but in order to see ourselves as we are and begin to remove the barriers that stand between each of us as individuals and our Christian neighbour whom we only occasionally *really* hear. In England we have a good chance of being able to modify and combine both the American understanding of techniques of learning in groups and the continental insistence on theological content.

It is in a situation of dialogue that we can become open with one another in the Church about some of the things that are impeding the teaching ministry. For example, how can we overcome the problem that the Bible is treated in one way when it is studied with the tools of scholarship and in another way when it is read as devotion? It is not two books, but we have two attitudes, and between the two we hardly know which is the real book. Do clergy take the laity sufficiently into their confidence on this matter and show how a more profound knowledge of Biblical meanings disclosed by scholarship makes it live both for devotion and for help in living?

Another need for openness is over questions of faith and doubt. In the small survey already referred to, a number of people said they were afraid to speak of their doubts or the muddle they were in over belief because they thought their clergy would be shocked. Others spoke of the need for help in prayer, but more than one 'didn't know how to ask for it'. Often a healthy distaste for exhibitionism and sentimentality prevents the upbuilding of the individual Christian by his coming to understand that even his doubts are not unique and that his Christian experience and faith can be validated, corrected and strengthened by others.

Where and how should such groups operate? There is room in the congregation for a group, or perhaps several, whose main purpose is study. This name will intimidate some. It is often wise to have a limited objective, such as a session of meetings over a short period or for a particular purpose. A strong disincentive to taking part in groups is the memory of one that trailed on, dwindling and growing more wordy. The educational machinery of a denomination exists to give help and advice. In such groups there will often be people who should be encouraged to take advantage of the extra-mural classes run by universities, the courses provided by local education authorities or in church centres. In the United States a number of theological colleges put on special courses for lay people which are not only well attended by the laity, but much appreciated by the teachers for the stimulus they give. We need many more better equipped lay people than we possess. The congregation as such cannot give the needed training and stimulus.

Neighbourhood groups are among the most exciting and promising developments in local church life. During the last war it was discovered that the effective neighbourhood, i.e. the area in which people know one another and act together, is very small—a single street, or even one side of a street. There are now a number of congregations in which this lesson has been learned and groups of members who happen to live close together are meeting regularly in their homes with neighbours who are not committed to a church. Many are groups of young parents. Much or little may come into these groups—fellowship and mutual help, discussion, study, worship. In at least one

Presbyterian church each neighbourhood group is cared for by an elder. Meeting in this way is often an important form of teaching ministry, both for those in the Church and for others. It is also a form of evangelism, better, often, if it does not set out to be so.

Three Basic Concerns

Worship, incorporation and teaching—these are three basic purposes for which we need an embodiment of the Church in a local congregation. They are the 'must' of our calling to come together as a Church. Many will regard these bases as, by themselves, inadequate. What about mission? Is not every local church called upon not just to support missions or conduct missions but to *be* mission? What about pastoral care? or fellowship? or service? What about all our existing or possible future church organizations for men or women or youth or children?

I am concerned about three things. *First: that the basic things get cluttered up and overlaid; we do too many things in many congregations and so produce in some people a sense of strain.* Duty rather than joy seems to keep a lot of things going. If we worshipped with the sense that this was the most wonderful privilege afforded to a Christian, and nurtured and cared for each baptized child or convert with the knowledge that each was a trust to the Church from God, what might not happen to us and our congregations? If these became our touchstones, how much of what we now do would we do with more joy, or else cease doing altogether?

I cannot get out of my mind the stubborn fact that after forty-five years of steady anti-God propaganda over thirty million Russians still go to church to worship God. None of the organizations or activities that to our way of thinking 'draw people into the Church' or keep them there are allowed. I am not saying that the Russian situation will hold for ever. I am certainly not saying that I would like to see such disabilities laid on us as are laid on them: God forbid. But I *am* saying that much as the churches in Russia have lost, they have left to them the two things that matter most—public worship and the Christian home—and they make the most of them.

My *second* concern is that *a great many of the things we struggle to do as a small congregation we could do more effectively on a much larger scale*. The Methodist circuit, or the deanery of a diocese, is often a far more fitting instrument than the congregation, and could be much more so if it conformed to the real social and geographical communities of today. But how many keen supporters of a local church regard the local church as 'we' and the larger unit as 'they'? The equipment and training of the laity needs resources beyond the congregation: the good boy of the parish, always at the vicar's right hand, is unfortunately too often the one who falls away at the university, his faith too tender a plant, his vision of the Church too parochial. We cannot tackle some of the big challenges to the Church today in housing estates, education, industry, except together across the boundaries of denominations, but few lay people receive any preparation for larger ventures of working together. Often it is the world in the form of the state school, the office or the voluntary organization, and not the Church, that gives them their contacts with Christians outside their own particular church. To co-operate needs far more than goodwill (though more of that would do no harm). It needs knowledge of what one believes and why; knowledge of the other; rootedness in a church where one belongs and is responsible, and on that basis full openness to others, without pretence and with humility. It needs responsibility, not only to one's own church as it is, but also towards that unity as yet unachieved for which Christ prayed and prays.

We have to take to heart a saying of Martin Buber, that the real quality of a community is revealed at its edges, where it meets other communities.

My *third* concern is that *many of the things that we regard as our rights as Christians we ought to be giving away to other people.* If Christian pastoral care has something about it not to be found in the same quality and manner in other forms of caring for human needs, then instead of regarding it as something we get from the Church, we laity should conceive of it as something we give. The author of the Epistle to the Hebrews has some sharp rebukes for those who had been long enough in the Church to be teachers, but are still asking to be taught; who won't tackle meat because milk is easier. If we were to regard pastoral care as something we give and receive in the mutuality of Christian fellowship—which we extend to, and even sometimes receive from, our non-Christian neighbours in the world—we would get rid of this attitude of claiming Christian rights and privileges for ourselves rather than others.

If Christian fellowship is a quality of value, why do we not give it away as lavishly as we can, wherever men and women come together? The answer to this question is very often that we are obsessively interested in people's joining and belonging to us. We ask of so many activities in which Christians take part 'will it bring people to church? Will they join our organization?' Should it not rather be our concern that people should respond to God's call exactly where they now are, and that his love and mercy should reach them in the midst of the world, in the high peaks of their joy and achievement as well as in their self-distrust or despair? Many of our efforts at trying to draw people into our company, our ways, our institutions, are in fact self-defeating, especially among youth. Young people shrewdly judge our faith by its performance in situations where we have not erected the stage and written the parts, where we show whether or not our concern is for *them*, or for getting them to do or be what we want.

Conclusion

This book began by saying that the Church is both the 'divine community' of Christ's foundation, the unbroken reality in heaven and on earth, and also a social institution. The heavenly treasure is within, and cannot be separated from, the earthly vessel. So long as we are in the body, the Church is a physical body, an institution. Instead of minimizing this fact we ought to be maximizing it *for the right ends*.

First, for the end of service: I have seen quite a lot of the work done by the churches for refugees. Many thousands of people now established as citizens in Australia, Brazil, Canada, the United States, and elsewhere, were once in camps and air-raid shelters, stateless, rightless, workless, hopeless. They owe their change of circumstance to the fact that the Church exists as an institution. The Church has directed outwards the organizing and money-raising powers of the institution and its ability to call on the service of its members at one end of the world to respond to the needs of the unseen, unknown neighbour at the other.

Second, for the end of creating for the lay person involved in the secular structures of the modern world the possibility of a rhythm of retreat for spiritual renewal alternating with involvement in, and identification with, the life of the world. Truly Christ is present in that world: but how can one recognize him and respond to him there if one does not know him in the fellowship and teaching of the institution?

Third, for the end of the Church's being in the world one of the few institutions which exists *for* man, and for all men, simply in order to raise a voice on man's behalf against his oppressors, detractors, corruptors and dividers.

So, as clergy and laity,
    as members of divided churches,
    as partners with all men in the toils and sufferings, the
        achievements and joys of the created world,
we look to Christ in whom all things are fulfilled, and say WE THE PEOPLE.